D0541101

JUST

5

INGREDIENTS

SLOW COOKER

An Hachette UK Company
www.hachette.co.uk

First published in Great Britain in 2015 by
Hamlyn, a division of Octopus Publishing Group Ltd
Endeavour House
189 Shaftesbury Avenue
London
WC2H 8JY

Copyright © Octopus Publishing Group Ltd 2015

All rights reserved. No part of this work may be reproduced or utilized in any form
or by any means, electronic or mechanical, including photocopying, recording or by
any information storage and retrieval system, without the prior written permission
of the publisher.

Some of the recipes in this book have previously appeared in other books published
by Hamlyn.

ISBN 978-0-60062-920-7

A CIP catalogue record for this book is available from the British Library

Printed and bound in China

10 9 8 7 6 5 4 3 2 1

Commissioning Editor Eleanor Maxfield
Editor Pauline Bache
Art Direction Geoff Fennell
Designer Abigail Read
Production Controller Sarah Kramer

Standard level spoon measurements are used in all recipes.
1 tablespoon = one 15 ml spoon
1 teaspoon = one 5 ml spoon

Both imperial and metric measurements have been given in all recipes. Use one set
of measurements only and not a mixture of both.

Milk should be full fat unless otherwise stated. Fresh herbs should be used unless
otherwise stated. Eggs should be medium unless otherwise stated.

The Department of Health advises that eggs should not be consumed raw. This
book contains dishes made with raw or lightly cooked eggs. It is prudent for more
vulnerable people such as pregnant and nursing mothers, invalids, the elderly, babies
and young children to avoid uncooked or lightly cooked dishes made with eggs. Once
prepared these dishes should be kept refrigerated and used promptly.

This book includes dishes made with nuts and nut derivatives. It is advisable for
customers with known allergic reactions to nuts and nut derivatives and those
who may be potentially vulnerable to these allergies, such as pregnant and nursing
mothers, invalids, the elderly, babies and children, to avoid dishes made with nuts
and nut oils. It is also prudent to check the labels of pre-prepared ingredients for
the possible inclusion of nut derivatives.

Read your slow cooker manual before you begin and if required, preheat the
slow cooker according to the manufacturer's instructions. Because slow cookers
vary slightly from manufacturer to manufacturer, check recipe timings with the
manufacturer's directions for a recipe using the same ingredients.

All recipes for this book were tested in oval-shaped slow cookers with a working
capacity of 2.5 litres (4 pints) and total capacity of 3.5 litres (6 pints) using metric
measurements. Where the slow cooker recipe is finished off under the grill, hold the
pot with tea towels to remove it from the machine housing

JUST

5

INGREDIENTS

SLOW COOKER

**MAKE LIFE SIMPLE WITH MORE THAN 100 RECIPES
USING 5 INGREDIENTS OR FEWER**

hamlyn

CONTENTS

INTRODUCTION

The recipes in this book have been chosen not only for their simplicity and great flavours, but also because they use just five or fewer main ingredients.

Applying a five-ingredient approach to cooking will help you create a repertoire of quick, easy adaptable dishes, that are not only cheap and tasty but that also require little shopping and preparation. You will learn to master some basic recipes in record time and learn to appreciate that cooking for yourself is a satisfying and empowering process.

This will make your life easier in three ways. First, because the recipes are straightforward there is less fiddly preparation, which will save you time. Second, you will find that shopping is simpler. How long do you really want to wander around a supermarket searching for something to cook? And third, it will save money. The five-ingredient approach will mean that you don't have a fridge full of half-used packets of strange ingredients, left over from previous meals that you will never use again.

Unlike other five-ingredient cookbooks, you won't have hundreds of hidden added extras to stock up on. This series requires you to remember 10 storecupboard extras only – simple, easy-to-remember basics you are likely to already have to hand.

Start by stocking up on your storecupboard ten (see page 11). Make sure you have at least some of them at all times so that you know you are just five ingredients away from a decent meal.

Next, choose a recipe that suits the time you have to cook, your energy levels and your mood. Check what storecupboard ingredients you will need on the list. The five key ingredients you will need to buy and complete the dish are clearly numbered.

One of the best ways to keep food costs down is to avoid expensive processed foods. Instead, buy basic ingredients such as vegetables, rice, pasta, fish and chicken, and build your meals around these. Buy food that lasts and to minimize waste plan around the lifetime dates of foods to avoid spending money on items that have to be thrown away. If you have a freezer, freeze the leftovers for another day.

Plan your meals for the week so you need to go shopping only once a week. When you get into the habit of doing this, the ingredients for each meal will be waiting when you need them.

Buy in bulk to get the best prices. Make time to shop around and compare prices in the nearest supermarket, online, your local shops and on market stalls to see which is cheapest. Stick to buying fruit and vegetables that are in season. Not only will they be better value than exotic produce flown in from abroad but you will be reducing your food miles. Finally, don't even think about spending precious cash on a supermarket's special offer unless it is something you will actually use. Three tins of pilchards in mustard sauce for the price of one is good value only if you are going to eat them.

If you want to prepare healthy, homely meals but think you don't have time, then think again. As little as 15–20 minutes spent early in the day are all you need to prepare supper to go into a slow cooker. Food that has slowly cooked has much more flavour than many dishes prepared in other ways.

Slow cookers are available in three sizes and are measured in capacity. For two people, choose one with a 1.5 litre (2½ pints) total capacity (working capacity 1 litre (1¾ pints)); for four people, you'll need a 3.5 litre (6 pints) total capacity (working capacity 2.5 litres (4 pints)) and for six people you'll need a larger size – 6.5 litres (11½ pints) total capacity, and working capacity of 4.5 litres (8 pints).

It is important to read the manufacturer's handbook before you start, since pre-heating instructions differ. You should only use your slow cooker with the addition of liquid, and ideally it should be no less than half full. Aim for the three-quarter full mark, and ensure that joints of meat take up no more than two-thirds of the space.

Surprisingly, the very large slow cookers cost very little more than the medium-sized ones, but because they have to be filled half-full, they may well be too big for your everyday needs. Oval-shaped models are the most versatile.

All slow cookers have High, Low, and off settings, and some have medium, warm or auto settings too. Sometimes a combination of settings can be the most effective.

Low settings should be used for diced meat and vegetable casseroles, chops or chicken joints, soups, rice dishes and fish dishes. High is good for sweet or savoury steamed puddings, whole chickens, lamb shoulders, pâtés and terrines.

You can adjust timings by changing heat settings using these guidelines:

Low	Medium	High
6–8 hours	4–6 hours	3–4 hours
8–10 hours	6–8 hours	5–6 hours
10–12 hours	8–10 hours	7–8 hours

Do not change timings or settings for fish, whole joints or dairy dishes.

When you use your slow cooker, position it on the work surface with the flex tucked away safely. The outside of the cooker gets hot so don't forget to wear oven gloves when handling the pot, and always set it on a heatproof mat.

Throughout this book there are recipes for all kinds of occasions – from food to share with friends to everyday basics, warming soups for lunch to cheap, filling end-of-the-month suppers.

WEEKLY PLANNER

ON A BUDGET

MONDAY
Tomato, Pepper & Garlic Bruschetta (see page 28)

TUESDAY
Chicken & Pesto Stew Pots (see page 106)

WEDNESDAY
Mushroom & Tomato Rigatoni (see page 94)

THURSDAY
Red Pepper & Chorizo Tortilla (see page 54)

FRIDAY
Sticky Jerk Ribs (see page 120)

SATURDAY
Chicken & Sweet Potato Balti (see page 74)

STORECUPBOARD 10

The only extras you will need!

1   Sugars
2   Flours
3   Oils & vinegars
4   Baking powder
5   Salt
6   Pepper
7   Stocks
8   Onion
9   Garlic
10 Lemon & lemon juice

SUNDAY
Toffee Apple Pancakes (see page 160)

SHOPPING LIST:

- 1 large red pepper
- 500 g (1 lb) plum tomatoes
- 1 large and 2 small carrots
- 350 g (12 oz) tenderstem broccoli
- 250 g (8 oz) cup mushrooms
- 250 g (8 oz) potatoes
- 375 g (12 oz) sweet potatoes
- 4 dessert apples
- 2–3 stems thyme
- bunch of fresh basil leaves
- bunch of fresh coriander
- 3 bay leaves
- 175 g (6 oz) French bread
- 2 naan breads
- 375 g (12 oz) pack or 6 ready-made pancakes
- 1.25 kg (2¼ lb) or 13 boneless, skinless chicken thighs
- 75 g (3 oz) chorizo, diced
- 1.25 kg (2½ lb) lean pork ribs
- 100 g (3½ oz) frozen peas
- vanilla ice cream
- 100 g (3½ oz) Parmesan cheese
- 6 eggs
- 150 ml (¼ pint) milk
- 50 g (2 oz) butter
- 250 g (8 oz) rigatoni
- 8 stoned black olives in brine
- 650 g (21 oz) tinned tomatoes
- 1 tablespoon tomato purée
- 100 g (3½ oz) roasted red pepper
- 100 g ready-made jerk glaze
- jar balti curry sauce
- 2 tablespoons golden syrup

WEEKLY PLANNER

SOMETHING TO CELEBRATE

MONDAY
Thai Coconut & Squash Soup (see page 40)

TUESDAY
Pot-roasted Chicken with Lemon (see page 102)

WEDNESDAY
Steak & Mushroom Pudding (see page 112)

THURSDAY
Aubergine Parmigiana (see page 98)

FRIDAY
Poached Salmon with Beurre Blanc (see page 72)

SATURDAY
Lemon & Poppy Seed Drizzle Cake (see page 146)

STORECUPBOARD 10

The only extras you will need!

1 Sugars
2 Flours
3 Oils & vinegars
4 Baking powder
5 Salt
6 Pepper
7 Stocks
8 Onion
9 Garlic
10 Lemon & lemon juice

SHOPPING LIST:

- 1 butternut squash, about 1 kg (2 lb)
- 3 carrots
- 3 celery sticks
- 100 g (3½ oz) cup mushrooms
- 800 g (26 oz) tomatoes
- 2 large aubergines
- small bunch of coriander
- small bunch of tarragon
- small bunch of basil
- 1 bay leaf
- bunch of chives
- small bunch of rosemary
- 1.5 kg (3 lb) whole chicken
- 700 g (1 lb 6 oz) rump steak
- 1–1.2 kg (2–2 lb 7 oz) half lamb shoulder on the bone
- 500 g (1 lb) piece of thick end salmon fillet
- 2 eggs
- 250 g (10½ oz) butter
- 170 g (6 oz) crème fraîche
- 75 g (3 oz) mature white cheese
- 2 tablespoons finely grated parmesan
- 2 tablespoons poppy seeds
- 4 teaspoons Thai red curry paste
- 1 teaspoon galangal paste
- 1 teaspoon Dijon mustard
- 2 tablespoons redcurrant jelly
- 250 ml (8 fl oz) carton coconut cream
- 150 g (5 oz) shredded suet
- 250 ml (8 fl oz) red wine
- 500 ml (17 fl oz) dry cider
- 200 ml (7 fl oz) dry white wine

SUNDAY
Pot-roasted Lamb with Rosemary (see page 80)

5 FOR VEGETARIANS

They may not be the first meals that come to mind with your slow cooker but these healthy feasts are perfect for vegetarians and meat-eaters alike.

Herby Stuffed Peppers (see page 52)

Braised Celery with Orange (see page 56)

Easy Cauliflower Dahl (see page 76)

Warm Beetroot & Bean Salad (see page 32)

Cauliflower & Spinach Balti (see page 110)

5 FOR ITALIAN INSPIRATION

Italian is the world's best-loved cuisine and these recipes showcase the fresh, punchy, indulgent flavours that we have all come to know and love.

Tomatoes Stuffed with Rice (see page 58)

Barley Risotto with Blue Cheese (see page 82)

Sausage Tagliatelle (see page 88)

Pepperonata (see page 90)

Balsamic Tomatoes with Spaghetti (see page 104)

5 FOR MEATY TREATS

From indulgent roasts to warming stews, slow cookers excell at drawing out the meaty richness in these delicious and simple dishes.

Beery Barley Beef (see page 62)

Winter Warming Lamb Pot Roast (see page 96)

Sausages with Yorkshire Pudding (see page 108)

Tamarind Beef with Ginger Beer (see page 70)

Balsamic Braised Pork Chops (see page 118)

5 FOR FRUITY FLAVOURS

Sweet, spicy, comforting and indulgent, these fruity treats are perfect for seeing through the long winter nights, all with just 5 ingredients.

Peaches with Marsala & Vanilla (see page 142)

Hot Toddy Oranges (see page 158)

Saffron Pears with Chocolate (see page 138)

Sticky Rum Bananas with Vanilla (see page 154)

Hot Spiced Berry Punch (see page 164)

5 FOR EASY BREAKFASTS

Prepare these delicious condiments in advance, or have a hearty breakfast waiting for you in the morning, these recipes prove that slow cooking is ideal for any time of day.

Apricot Conserve (see page 182)

Banana & Cinnamon Porridge (see page 24)

Orange Marmalade (see page 178)

Blackberry & Apple Jam (see page 188)

Breakfast Baked Tomatoes (see page 34)

5 FOR FISH & SEAFOOD

From refreshing summer dishes to warming winter treats, fish and seafood are so versatile and easy to prepare when you only need 5 key ingredients.

Tapenade Crusted Cod (see page 64)

Baked Seafood Tagliatelle (see page 68)

Hot Soused Herrings (see page 84)

Smoked Cod with Bean Mash (see page 100)

Smoked Salmon Timbales (see page 42)

LIGHT
BITES

SERVES 2

Preparation time 5 minutes
Cooking temperature High
Cooking time 1–1¼ hours

INGREDIENTS

1	**2 eggs**
2	**few fresh chopped chives**
3	**2 smoked haddock steaks, each 125 g (4 oz), defrosted if frozen**
4	**125 g (4 oz) young spinach**
5	**5 g (¼ oz) butter**

STORECUPBOARD

1 tablespoon sunflower oil; salt and black pepper; 450 ml (¾ pint) boiling water

Breakfast Poached Eggs & Haddock

■ Preheat the slow cooker if necessary, see manufacturer's instructions. Cover the inside of 2 ovenproof ramekins or metal pudding moulds with a little sunflower oil then break an egg into each dish and sprinkle the top with a little salt and pepper and a few chives.

■ Set the egg dishes in the centre of the slow cooker, then add the fish steaks to either side. Pour the boiling water over the fish so that the water comes halfway up the sides of the dishes.

■ Cover with the lid and cook on High for 1–1¼ hours or until the eggs are done to your liking and the fish flakes easily when pressed with a fork.

■ Rinse the spinach with a little water, drain and put in a microwave-proof dish, cover and cook in the microwave on full power for 1 minute until just wilted. Spoon on to two serving plates, lift out the fish with a draining spoon, place on top of the spinach. Lift the egg dishes out with ovengloves, loosen the eggs with a knife and put on top of the fish. Dot with the butter and serve.

TRY IT WITH SALMON

For breakfast poached eggs with salmon, add the eggs to the dishes as for the main recipe then add 2 x 125 g (4 oz) salmon steaks to the slow cooker pot, pour over the boiling water and cook as for the main recipe. Arrange two sliced tomatoes on two serving plates, top with the cooked and drained salmon, then the eggs and a tiny dot of butter.

SERVES 4

Preparation time 5 minutes
Cooking temperature Low
Cooking time 1–2 hours

INGREDIENTS

1 300 ml (½ pint) UHT milk

2 150 g (5 oz) porridge oats

3 2 bananas

4 ¼ teaspoon ground cinnamon

STORECUPBOARD

600 ml (1 pint) boiling water; 4 tablespoons light
or dark muscovado sugar

Banana & Cinnamon Porridge

■ Preheat the slow cooker if necessary,
see manufacturer's instructions. Pour the
boiling water and milk into the slow cooker
pot, then stir in the oats.

■ Cover with the lid and cook on Low for
1 hour for 'runny' porridge or 2 hours for
'thick' porridge.

■ Spoon the porridge into bowls, slice
the bananas and divide among the bowls.
Mix together the sugar and cinnamon and
sprinkle over the top.

TRANSFORM IT INTO MUESLI

For hot spiced muesli, follow the main recipe, adding 175 g (6 oz) Swiss-style muesli. When cooked, stir in ¼ teaspoon ground cinnamon and top with 100 g (3½ oz) diced dried apricots. Drizzle over 2 tablespoons honey before serving.

Preparation time 20 minutes
Cooking temperature Low and High
Cooking time 6¼ hours–8 hours 20 minutes

INGREDIENTS

1 150 g (5 oz) chorizo, skinned and diced

2 625 g (1¼ lb) or 3 small baking potatoes, cut into 1 cm (½ inch) dice

3 1 teaspoon smoked paprika (pimenton)

4 125 g (4 oz) green cabbage, finely shredded

STORECUPBOARD

2 tablespoons olive oil; 2 onions, chopped; 2 garlic cloves, finely chopped; 1.2 litres (2 pints) hot chicken stock; salt and black pepper

Caldo Verde

■ Preheat the slow cooker if necessary, see manufacturer's instructions. Heat the oil in a large frying pan, add the onions and fry, stirring, for 5 minutes or until lightly browned. Add the garlic, chorizo, potatoes and paprika and cook for 2 minutes.

■ Transfer the mixture to the slow cooker pot, add the hot stock and season to taste with salt and pepper. Cover with the lid and cook on Low for 6–8 hours.

■ Add the cabbage, replace the lid and cook on High for 15–20 minutes or until the cabbage is tender. Ladle the soup into bowls and serve.

ADD PUMPKIN

For caldo verde with pumpkin, prepare the soup as for the main recipe, reducing the potatoes to 375 g (12 oz) and adding 250 g (8 oz) peeled, deseeded and diced pumpkin. Reduce the chicken stock to 900 ml (1½ pints) and add a 400 g (13 oz) can chopped tomatoes.

Preparation time 20 minutes
Cooking temperature High
Cooking time 3–5 hours

INGREDIENTS

1   1 large red pepper, quartered, cored, deseeded

2   500 g (1 lb) plum tomatoes, halved

3   2–3 stems thyme

4   8 slices French bread, 175 g (6 oz)

5   8 stoned black olives in brine, drained

STORECUPBOARD

4 large garlic cloves, unpeeled; 2 teaspoons caster sugar; 1 tablespoon virgin olive oil; salt and black pepper

Tomato, Pepper & Garlic Bruschetta

■ Preheat the slow cooker if necessary, see manufacturer's instructions. Arrange the peppers, skin side downwards in the base of the slow cooker pot, arrange the tomatoes on top then tuck the garlic in and around the tomatoes.

■ Tear the leaves from the thyme stems and scatter over the tomatoes, sprinkle the sugar on top, drizzle with the oil then add salt and pepper. Cover and cook on High for 3–5 hours until tender and the tomatoes still hold their shape.

■ Lift the vegetables out of the slow cooker pot with a draining spoon. Peel the skins away from the peppers, tomatoes and garlic then roughly chop and mix together. Add a little extra salt and pepper if needed.

■ Toast the bread on both sides, arrange on a serving plate then spoon the tomato mix on top. Garnish each with an olive and serve as a light lunch or starter.

SERVES 4

Preparation time 20 minutes
Cooking temperature Low
Cooking time 6–8 hours

INGREDIENTS

1	150 g (5 oz) chorizo, skinned and diced
2	2–3 stems thyme plus extra thyme leaves, to garnish
3	1 tablespoon tomato purée
4	375 g (12 oz) sweet potatoes, diced
5	410 g (13½ oz) can chickpeas, drained

STORECUPBOARD

2 tablespoons olive oil; 1 onion, chopped; 2 garlic cloves, finely chopped; 1 litre (1¾ pint) chicken stock; salt and black pepper

Chunky Chickpea & Chorizo Soup

■ Preheat the slow cooker if necessary, see manufacturer's instructions. Heat the oil in a frying pan, add the onion and fry, stirring, for 5 minutes or until just beginning to turn golden in colour.

■ Stir in the garlic and chorizo and cook for 2 minutes. Add the thyme, stock and tomato purée and bring to the boil, stirring, then add a little salt and pepper.

■ Add the sweet potatoes and chickpeas to the slow cooker pot and pour over the hot stock mixture. Cover with the lid and cook on Low for 6–8 hours until the sweet potatoes are tender.

■ Ladle into bowls, sprinkle with a little chopped extra thyme and serve.

TRY IT WITH FRESH TOMATOES

For tomato, chickpea & chorizo
soup, make the soup up to the point
where the thyme and stock have
been added. Reduce to 75 ml (1¼
pints) and add to the frying
pan with the tomato purée and
2 teaspoons brown sugar. Bring to
the boil. Replace the sweet potatoes
with 500 g (1 lb) skinned and diced
tomatoes along with the chickpeas.
Pour over the stock mixture and
continue as for the main recipe.

Preparation time 25 minutes
Cooking temperature Low
Cooking time 3½–4½ hours

INGREDIENTS

1	500 g (1 lb) raw beetroot, peeled and finely diced
2	2 x 410 g (13½ oz) cans borlotti beans, rinsed and drained
3	200 g (7 oz) natural yogurt
4	1 cos or iceberg lettuce
5	4 tablespoons chopped fresh coriander leaves

STORECUPBOARD

1 tablespoon olive oil; 1 large onion, chopped; 450 ml (¾ pint) vegetable stock; salt and black pepper

Warm Beetroot & Bean Salad

■ Preheat the slow cooker if necessary, see manufacturer's instructions. Heat the oil in a frying pan, add the onion and fry, stirring, for 5 minutes or until pale golden. Add the beetroot to the pan with the drained beans, stock and plenty of salt and pepper. Bring to the boil, stirring.

■ Transfer the beetroot mixture to the slow cooker pot. Cover with the lid and cook on Low for 3½–4½ hours or until the beetroot is tender. Stir well and lift the pot out of the cooker.

■ Stir the yogurt and season with salt and pepper. Arrange the lettuce leaves on 4-5 individual plates. Top with the warm beetroot salad, then add spoonfuls of the yogurt. Scatter the coriander over the top and serve at once.

MAKE A FETA VERSION

For warm beetroot salad with feta & tomatoes, prepare the beetroot and beans as for the main recipe. Mix 125 g (4 oz) crumbled feta cheese with 2 diced tomatoes. Core, deseed and dice ½ red or orange pepper and combine with the cheese and tomatoes. Add 4 tablespoons chopped mint and 2 tablespoons olive oil. Spoon over the salad and top with 50 g (2 oz) rocket leaves.

Preparation time 10 minutes
Cooking temperature Low
Cooking time 8–10 hours

INGREDIENTS

1   **500 g (1 lb) plum tomatoes, halved lengthways, no need to peel**

2   **2–3 stems fresh thyme**

3   **4 slices wholewheat bread, each 40 g (1½ oz)**

4   **little chopped parsley, optional**

STORECUPBOARD

1 tablespoon balsamic vinegar; salt and black pepper

Breakfast Baked Tomatoes

■ Preheat the slow cooker if necessary, see manufacturer's instructions. Arrange the tomatoes cut side uppermost and packed closely together in a single layer in the slow cooker pot, to get them in you may have to stand them slightly on their sides.

■ Tear the thyme leaves from the stems and sprinkle over the tomatoes. Drizzle with the balsamic vinegar then season with salt and pepper.

■ Cover with the lid and cook on Low for 8–10 hours overnight. Next morning make the toast, arrange on serving plates and top with the tomatoes and a little of the juice. Sprinkle with a little chopped parsley, if liked.

MAKE A SPAGHETTI SAUCE

For balsamic tomatoes with spaghetti, cook the tomatoes as for the main recipe, but during the day, then chop and mix with the cooking juices. Cook 300 g (10 oz) dried spaghetti according to the packet instructions. Drain and toss with the tomatoes. Sprinkle with 1 tablespoon freshly grated parmesan per portion.

Preparation time 10 minutes
Cooking temperature High
Cooking time 5 hours 20 minutes–7½ hours

INGREDIENTS

1   1 chicken carcass

2   2 celery sticks, sliced

3   1 bouquet garni

4   75 g (3 oz) vermicelli pasta

5   4 tablespoons chopped parsley

STORECUPBOARD

1 onion, cut into wedges; 1.25 litres (2¼ pints)
boiling water; salt and black pepper

Chicken & Noodle Broth

■ Preheat the slow cooker if necessary, see manufacturer's instructions. Put the chicken carcass into the slow cooker pot, breaking it into 2 pieces if necessary to make it fit. Add the onion, celery and bouquet garni.

■ Pour over the boiling water and add a little salt and pepper. Cover with the lid and cook on High for 5–7 hours.

■ Strain the soup into a large sieve, then quickly pour the hot soup back into the slow cooker pot. Take any meat off the carcass and add to the pot. Taste and adjust the seasoning if needed. Add the pasta and cook on High for 20–30 minutes or until the pasta is just cooked. Sprinkle with parsley and ladle into deep bowls.

MAKE IT CREAMY

For creamy chicken soup, make the soup base as for the main recipe, strain and pour it back into the slow cooker. Add 200 g (7 oz) finely sliced leeks and cook on High for 30 minutes. Mash or purée with a stick blender, then stir in 150 g (5 oz) mascarpone cheese until melted. Ladle into bowls and sprinkle with extra mint leaves, if liked.

Preparation time 30 minutes, plus overnight chilling
Cooking temperature High
Cooking time 5–6 hours

INGREDIENTS

1 200 g (7 oz) smoked streaky bacon rashers

2 115 g (3¾ oz) pack dried orange and cranberry stuffing mix

3 25 g (1 oz) dried cranberries

4 500 g (1 lb) skinless turkey breast steaks

5 1 egg, beaten

STORECUPBOARD

1 tablespoon sunflower oil, plus extra for greasing; 1 onion, finely chopped; salt and black pepper

Turkey & Cranberry Meatloaf

■ Preheat the slow cooker if necessary, see manufacturer's instructions. Lightly oil a loaf tin, 14 cm (5½ inches) in diameter and 9 cm (3½ inches) high, and base-line with nonstick baking paper, checking first that the dish will fit in the slow cooker pot. Stretch each bacon rasher with the flat of a large cook's knife, until half as long again, and use about three-quarters of the rashers to line the base and sides of the dish, trimming to fit.

■ Put the stuffing mix in a bowl, add the cranberries and mix with boiling water according to the pack instructions. Heat the oil in a frying pan, add the onion and fry for 5 minutes, stirring, until softened. Set aside. Finely chop the turkey slices in a food processor or pass through a coarse mincer.

■ Mix the stuffing with the fried onion, chopped turkey and egg. Season well and spoon into the bacon-lined dish. Press flat and cover with the remaining bacon rashers. Cover the top of the dish with foil and lower into the slow cooker pot. Pour boiling water into the pot to come halfway up the sides of the dish. Cover with the lid and cook on High for 5–6 hours or until the juices run clear when the centre of the meatloaf is pierced with a knife.

■ Lift the dish out of the slow cooker pot using a tea towel and leave to cool. Transfer to the refrigerator to chill overnight until firm. Loosen the edge of the meatloaf with a knife, turn out on to a plate and peel off the lining paper. Cut into thick slices and serve with salad and spoonfuls of cranberry sauce, if liked.

Preparation time 20 minutes
Cooking temperature Low
Cooking time 7-8 hours

INGREDIENTS

1   4 teaspoons Thai red curry paste

2   1 teaspoon galangal paste

3   1 butternut squash, about 1 kg (2 lb), peeled, deseeded and cut into 2 cm (¾ inch) chunks

4   250 ml (8 fl oz) carton coconut cream

5   small bunch of coriander

STORECUPBOARD

1 tablespoon sunflower oil; 1 onion, chopped; 2 garlic cloves, finely chopped; 750 ml (1¼ pint) vegetable stock; salt and black pepper

Thai Coconut & Squash Soup

■ Preheat the slow cooker if necessary, see manufacturer's instructions. Heat the oil in a large frying pan, add the onion and fry until softened. Stir in the curry paste, galangal and garlic and cook for 1 minute, then mix in the squash.

■ Pour in the coconut cream and stock, and bring to the boil, stirring. Pour into the slow cooker pot, cover with the lid and cook on Low for 7-8 hours or until the squash is tender. (You may find that the coconut cream separates slightly but this will disappear after puréeing.)

■ Purée the soup while still in the slow cooker pot with a stick blender. Alternatively, transfer to a liquidizer and purée, in batches if necessary, until smooth, then return it to the slow cooker pot and reheat on High for 15 minutes.

■ Reserve a few sprigs of coriander for garnish, chop the rest and stir into the soup. Ladle the soup into bowls and garnish with the reserved coriander sprigs.

ADD AN ORANGE TWIST

For squash & orange soup, fry
the onion in 25 g (1 oz) butter, then
add the diced butternut squash
with the grated rind and juice of
2 small oranges, 900 ml (1½ pints)
vegetable stock and 3 whole star
anise. Bring to the boil, stirring, add
a little salt and pepper and continue
as for the main recipe. Remove
the star anise before puréeing and
serve with swirls of double cream,
omitting the coriander.

Preparation time 30 minutes, plus chilling
Cooking temperature Low
Cooking time 3–3½ hours

INGREDIENTS

1 butter for greasing

2 200 ml (7 fl oz) full-fat crème fraîche

3 4 egg yolks

4 1 small growing pot of basil

5 100 g (3½ oz) sliced smoked salmon

STORECUPBOARD

grated rind and juice of ½ lemon, plus lemon
wedges, to garnish; salt and black pepper

Smoked Salmon Timbales

■ Preheat the slow cooker if necessary, see manufacturer's instructions. Lightly butter 4 individual metal moulds, each 150 ml (¼ pint), and base-line with circles of nonstick baking or greaseproof paper.

■ Put the crème fraîche in a bowl and gradually beat in the egg yolks. Add the lemon rind and juice and season with salt and pepper. Chop half of the basil and 75 g (3 oz) of the smoked salmon, then stir both into the crème fraîche mixture.

■ Pour the mixture into the prepared moulds. Stand the moulds in the slow cooker pot (there is no need to cover them with foil). Pour hot water around the moulds to come halfway up the sides, cover with the lid and cook on Low for 3–3½ hours or until the moulds are set.

■ Remove the moulds carefully from the slow cooker using a tea towel and leave to cool at room temperature. Transfer to the refrigerator and chill for at least 4 hours or overnight if possible.

■ To serve, loosen the edges of the timbales with a knife dipped in hot water, then invert on to serving plates and remove the moulds. Smooth any rough areas with the side of the knife and remove the lining discs. Top with the remaining smoked salmon and basil leaves and garnish with lemon wedges.

TRY IT WITH MACKEREL

For smoked mackerel timbales, omit the basil and smoked salmon and stir in 3 tablespoons freshly chopped chives, ½ teaspoon hot horseradish and 75 g (3 oz) skinned, flaked smoked mackerel fillets. Continue as for the main recipe.

SERVES 4–6

Preparation time 15 minutes
Cooking temperature High
Cooking time 2½–3 hours

INGREDIENTS

1	1 red pepper, cored, deseeded and diced
2	750 g (1½ lb) tomatoes, roughly chopped
3	1 tablespoon tomato purée
4	4 tablespoons of ready-made pesto

STORECUPBOARD

2 tablespoons olive oil; 1 onion, chopped; 1 garlic clove, finely chopped; 600 ml (1 pint) vegetable stock; 2 teaspoons caster sugar; 1 tablespoon balsamic vinegar, plus extra to garnish; salt and black pepper

Tomato & Red Pepper Soup

■ Preheat the slow cooker if necessary, see manufacturer's instructions. Heat the oil in a large frying pan, add the onion and fry until softened. Stir in the red pepper, tomatoes and garlic and fry for 1–2 minutes.

■ Pour in the stock and add the tomato purée, sugar, vinegar and a little salt and pepper and bring to the boil, stirring. Pour into the slow cooker pot, cover with the lid and cook on High for 2½–3 hours or until the vegetables are tender.

■ Purée the soup while still in the slow cooker pot with a stick blender. Alternatively, transfer to a liquidizer and purée, in batches if necessary, until smooth, then return to the slow cooker pot and reheat on High for 15 minutes.

■ Taste and adjust the seasoning, if needed, then ladle the soup into bowls Garnish with a drizzle of extra vinegar and stir in spoonfuls of pesto.

A HOME-MADE PESTO GARNISH

For spring onion & basil pesto, roughly chop 4 spring onions, then finely chop using a blender or liquidizer with 25 g (1 oz) freshly grated Parmesan, 4 sprigs basil, 4 tablespoons olive oil and a pinch pepper until a coarse paste. Spoon over the soup just before serving.

SERVES 4

Preparation time 30 minutes, plus cooling and overnight chilling
Cooking temperature High
Cooking time 5–6 hours

INGREDIENTS

1 2 duck legs

2 500 g (1 lb) rindless belly pork rashers, halved

3 1 sharp dessert apple, such as Granny Smith, peeled, cored and thickly sliced

4 2–3 sprigs of thyme

5 150 ml (¼ pint) dry cider

STORECUPBOARD

1 onion, cut into wedges; 250 ml (8 fl oz) chicken stock; salt and black pepper

Duck, Pork & Apple Rillettes

■ Preheat the slow cooker if necessary, see manufacturer's instructions. Put the duck and belly pork into the base of the slow cooker pot. Tuck the onion and apple between the pieces of meat and add the thyme.

■ Pour the stock and cider into a saucepan and add plenty of salt and pepper. Bring to the boil, then pour into the slow cooker pot. Cover with the lid and cook on High for 5–6 hours or until the duck and pork are cooked through and tender.

■ Lift the meat out of the slow cooker pot with a slotted spoon and transfer to a large plate, then leave to cool for 30 minutes. Peel away the duck skin and remove the bones. Shred the meat into small pieces and discard the thyme sprigs. Scoop out the apple and onion with a slotted spoon, finely chop and mix with the meat, then taste and adjust the seasoning, if needed.

■ Pack the chopped meat mix into 4 individual dishes or small 'le parfait' jars and press down firmly. Spoon over the juices from the slow cooker pot to cover and seal the meat. Leave to cool, then transfer to the refrigerator and chill well.

■ When the fat has solidified on the top, cover each dish with a lid or clingfilm and store in the refrigerator for up to 1 week. Serve the rillettes with warm crusty bread, a few radishes and pickled shallots, if liked.

USE CHICKEN AND PRUNE

For chicken, pork & prune rillettes, omit the duck and put 2 chicken legs into the slow cooker pot with the belly pork rashers, onion and thyme, replacing the apple with 75 g (3 oz) ready-to-eat stoned prunes. Continue as for the main recipe.

SERVES 4

Preparation time 25 minutes
Cooking temperature Low
Cooking time 4–5 hours

INGREDIENTS

1 25 g (1 oz) butter

2 250 ml (8 fl oz) brown ale

3 1 tablespoon Worcestershire sauce, plus 2 teaspoons

4 8 slices of French bread

5 75 g (3 oz) mature Cheddar cheese, grated

STORECUPBOARD

2 tablespoons olive oil; 500 g (1 lb) onions, thinly sliced; 1 tablespoon caster sugar; 2 tablespoons plain flour; 750 ml (1¼ pints) beef stock; salt and black pepper

Caramelized Onion Soup

■ Preheat the slow cooker if necessary, see manufacturer's instructions. Heat the butter and oil in a large frying pan, add the onions and fry over a medium heat, stirring occasionally, for 15 minutes or until softened and just beginning to turn golden. Add the sugar and fry for 10 minutes, stirring frequently as the onions begin to caramelize and turn a deep golden brown.

■ Stir in the flour, then add the ale, stock and 1 tablespoon of the Worcestershire sauce. Add a little salt and pepper and bring to the boil, stirring. Pour into the slow cooker pot, cover with the lid and cook on Low for 4–5 hours or until the onions are very soft.

■ When almost ready to serve, toast the French bread slices on both sides, sprinkle with the cheese and drizzle with the remaining Worcestershire sauce. Grill until the cheese is bubbling. Ladle the soup into shallow bowls and float the croutes on top.

MAKE IT FRENCH

For French onion soup, fry the onions as for the main recipe and stir in the flour. Replace the ale with 250 ml (8 fl oz) red wine and add with the stock, bay leaves and salt and pepper, omitting the Worcestershire sauce. Continue as for the main recipe. For the croutes, rub one side of the toasted bread with a cut garlic clove, sprinkle with 75 g (3 oz) grated Gruyère and grill. Serve as for the main recipe.

SERVES 4

Preparation time 20 minutes
Cooking temperature Low
Cooking time 6–8 hours

INGREDIENTS

1 1 aubergine, sliced

2 1 teaspoon ground cumin

3 125 g (4 oz) red lentils

4 400 g (13 oz) can chopped tomatoes

5 chopped coriander, to garnish

STORECUPBOARD

4 tablespoons olive oil, plus extra to garnish; 1 onion, chopped; 2 garlic cloves, finely chopped; 750 ml (1¼ pints) boiling vegetable stock; salt and black pepper

Tomato, Lentil & Aubergine Soup

■ Preheat the slow cooker if necessary, see manufacturer's instructions. Heat 1 tablespoon of the oil in a large frying pan, add one-third of the aubergines and fry on both sides until softened and golden. Scoop out of the pan with a slotted spoon and transfer to a plate. Repeat with the rest of the aubergines using 2 more tablespoons of oil.

■ Add the remaining oil to the pan and fry the onion for 5 minutes or until softened. Stir in the garlic and cumin and cook for a further minute, then mix in the lentils and tomatoes. Add a little salt and pepper and bring to the boil. Pour the mixture into the slow cooker pot and stir in the boiling stock.

■ Cover with the lid and cook on Low for 6–8 hours. Serve the soup as it is or purée it with a stick blender, if preferred. Ladle the soup into bowls, drizzle with a little extra olive oil and sprinkle with coriander.

MAKE IT SPANISH

For tomato, lentil & chorizo soup, omit the aubergine and fry the onion in 1 tablespoon olive oil. Add the garlic, paprika and ground cumin, then stir in 1 cored, deseeded and diced red pepper and 50 g (2 oz) diced chorizo. Fry for 2 minutes and continue as for the main recipe.

SERVES 4

Preparation time 20 minutes
Cooking temperature Low
Cooking time 4–5 hours

INGREDIENTS

1	**4 different coloured peppers**
2	**100 g (3½ oz) easy-cook brown rice**
3	**410 g (13½ oz) can chickpeas, drained**
4	**small bunch of parsley, roughly chopped**
5	**small bunch of mint, roughly chopped**

STORECUPBOARD

1 onion, finely chopped; 2 garlic cloves, finely
chopped; 600 ml (1 pint) boiling vegetable stock;
salt and black pepper

Herby Stuffed Peppers

■ Preheat the slow cooker if necessary,
see manufacturer's instructions. Cut the
top off each pepper, then remove the core
and seeds.

■ Mix together the rice, chickpeas, herbs,
onion, garlic and plenty of salt and pepper
in a bowl. Spoon the mixture into the
peppers, then put the peppers into the
slow cooker pot.

■ Pour the hot stock around the peppers,
cover with the lid and cook on Low for
4–5 hours or until the rice and peppers are
tender. Spoon into dishes and serve.

SPICE IT UP

For chilli stuffed peppers, fry the onion in 1 tablespoon olive oil until softened. Stir in the garlic and ½ teaspoon each of hot paprika or chilli powder, ground allspice, and ground cumin. Mix with the brown rice and a drained 410 g (13½ oz) can red kidney beans instead of the chickpeas and herbs. Spoon into the peppers and put into the slow cooker. Stir 2 tablespoons tomato puree into the stock and continue as for the main recipe.

SERVES 4

Preparation time 20 minutes
Cooking temperature High
Cooking time 2–2½ hours

INGREDIENTS

1	75 g (3 oz) chorizo, diced
2	6 eggs
3	150 ml (¼ pint) milk
4	100 g (3½ oz) roasted red pepper (from a jar), drained and sliced
5	250 g (8 oz) cooked potatoes, sliced

STORECUPBOARD

1 tablespoon olive oil, plus extra for greasing;
1 small onion, chopped; salt and black pepper

Red Pepper & Chorizo Tortilla

■ Preheat the slow cooker if necessary, see manufacturer's instructions. Lightly oil a 1.2 litre (2 pint) soufflé dish and base-line with a circle of nonstick baking paper, checking first that the dish will fit in the slow cooker pot.

■ Heat the oil in a frying pan, add the onion and chorizo and fry for 4–5 minutes or until the onion has softened. Beat the eggs, milk and a little salt and pepper in a bowl, then add the onion and chorizo, the red pepper and sliced potatoes and mix together.

■ Tip the mixture into the oiled dish, cover the top with foil and stand the dish in the slow cooker pot. Pour boiling water into the pot to come halfway up the sides of the dish. Cover with the lid and cook on High for 2–2½ hours or until the egg mixture has set in the centre.

■ Lift the dish out of the slow cooker pot using a tea towel and remove the foil. Loosen the edge of the tortilla with a knife, turn it out on to a plate and peel off the lining paper. Cut into slices and serve hot or cold.

MAKE IT CHEESY

For cheesy bacon & rosemary tortilla, replace the chorizo with 75 g (3 oz) diced smoked streaky bacon and fry with the onion. Beat the eggs and milk in a bowl with chopped leaves from 2 small rosemary sprigs, 4 tablespoons freshly grated Parmesan or Cheddar and salt and pepper. Replace the red pepper with 75 g (3 oz) sliced button mushrooms and continue as for the main recipe.

SERVES 4-6

Preparation time 10 minutes
Cooking temperature High
Cooking time 4–5 hours

INGREDIENTS

1   **2 celery hearts**

2   **grated rind and juice of 1 small orange**

3   **400 g (13 oz) can chopped tomatoes**

STORECUPBOARD

2 tablespoons light muscovado sugar; salt
and black pepper

Braised Celery with Orange

■ Preheat the slow cooker if necessary,
see manufacturer's instructions. Cut each
celery heart in half lengthways, then rinse
under the cold tap to remove any traces of
dirt. Drain and put into the slow cooker pot.

■ Mix the remaining ingredients together
and pour over the celery. Cover with the lid
and cook on High for 4–5 hours or until the
celery is tender. If you would prefer a thicker
sauce, pour off the liquid from the slow
cooker pot into a saucepan and boil rapidly
for 4–5 minutes to reduce. Pour back over
the celery and serve.

TRY A NEW VEGETABLE

For braised fennel with orange, cut 3 small fennel bulbs into halves, add to the slow cooker pot with the remaining ingredients and cook as for the main recipe. Sprinkle the top with 50 g (2 oz) torn ciabatta bread fried in 2 tablespoons olive oil until crisp and golden.

Preparation time 15 minutes, plus standing
Cooking temperature Low
Cooking time 4–5 hours

INGREDIENTS

1   **4 large or 8 small tomatoes, about 625 g (1¼ lb) in total**

2   **75 g (3 oz) arborio, carnaroli or vialone nano rice**

3   **6 basil leaves, torn**

STORECUPBOARD

2 garlic cloves, crushed; 2 tablespoons extra virgin olive oil, plus extra for oiling and drizzling; salt and black pepper

Tomatoes Stuffed with Rice

■ Preheat the slow cooker if necessary, see manufacturer's instructions. Cut the top off each tomato, then scoop out the pulp and chop. Transfer to a large bowl, taking care not to lose any of the tomato juices, and add the garlic, rice and basil. Season with salt and pepper and stir in 1 tablespoon of the oil. Cover and leave to stand at room temperature for 1 hour, for the rice to soak up all the juices.

■ Stuff the tomatoes with the rice mixture, then transfer into the slow cooker pot. Top with their reserved lids and drizzle with the remaining oil.

■ Cover with the lid and cook on Low for 4–5 hours or until the rice and tomatoes are tender. Spoon into dishes and serve.

HEARTY
SUPPERS

SERVES 4

Preparation time 15 minutes
Cooking temperature Low
Cooking time 9–10 hours

INGREDIENTS

1	625 g (1¼ lb) lean stewing beef, cubed
2	500 g (8 oz) mixed root vegetables such as carrots, parsnips or potatoes, diced
3	300 ml (½ pint) light ale
4	dried bouquet garni
5	100 g (3½ oz) pearl barley

STORECUPBOARD

1 tablespoon sunflower oil; 1 onion, chopped; 1 tablespoon plain flour; 750 ml (1¼ pint) beef stock; salt and black pepper

Beery Barley Beef

■ Preheat the slow cooker if necessary, see manufacturer's instructions. Heat the oil in a frying pan, add the beef a few pieces at a time, then fry over a high heat, stirring, until browned. Remove the beef with a slotted spoon and transfer to the slow cooker pot.

■ Add the onion to the frying pan and fry, stirring, for 5 minutes or until lightly browned. Mix in the flour, then add the root vegetables and beer and bring to the boil, stirring. Pour into the slow cooker pot.

■ Add the stock to the frying pan with the bouquet garni and a little salt and pepper, bring to the boil, then pour into the slow cooker pot. Add the pearl barley, cover with the lid and cook on Low for 9–10 hours until the beef is tender.

PREPARE AN ACCOMPANIMENT

To make herb croutons, beat
2 tablespoons chopped parsley,
2 tablespoons chopped chives and
1 tablespoon chopped tarragon and
a little black pepper into 75 g (3 oz)
soft butter. Thickly slice ½ French
stick, toast lightly on both sides,
then spread with the herb butter.

Preparation time 15 minutes
Cooking temperature Low
Cooking time 3½–4 hours

INGREDIENTS

| 1 | 375 g (6 oz) tomatoes, roughly chopped (no need to peel), plus juice included |

| 2 | 200 g (7 oz) spinach, rinsed, drained |

| 3 | 4 cod steaks, each 150 g (5 oz), skinned |

| 4 | 200 g (7 oz) can stuffed green olives with hot pimento in brine, drained weight 85 g (3 oz) |

| 5 | 50 g (2 oz) chorizo, diced |

STORECUPBOARD

salt and black pepper

Tapenade Crusted Cod

■ Preheat the slow cooker if necessary, see manufacturer's instructions. Spoon the tomato juice over the base of the slow cooker pot, then add the spinach and tomatoes in an even layer. Season with salt and pepper. Arrange the fish steaks on top in a single layer and season these too.

■ Finely chop or blitz the drained olives in a food processor with the chorizo. Spread over the cod steaks, then cover with the lid and cook on Low for 3½–4 hours until the fish steaks are bright white and break easily into flakes when pressed with a fork.

■ Lift out of the slow cooker pot with a fish slice and transfer to serving plates.

SERVES 4

Preparation time 30 minutes
Cooking temperature High
Cooking time 4–5 hours

INGREDIENTS

1	2 x 240 g (8½ oz) packs of Quorn sausages
2	1 tablespoon tomato purée
3	2 teaspoons wholegrain mustard
4	625 g (1½ lb) floury potatoes
5	675 g (1 lb 6 oz) green beans

STORECUPBOARD

1½ tablespoons sunflower oil; 300 g (10 oz) onion, halved, thinly sliced; 2 teaspoons dark muscovado sugar; 350 ml (12 fl oz) vegetable stock; 2 teaspoons cornflour; salt and black pepper

Quorn Sausages with Onion Gravy

■ Preheat the slow cooker if necessary, see manufacturer's instructions. Heat a tablespoon of the sunflower oil in a large frying pan, then add the sausages and cook until browned all over. Take out of the pan and put on a plate.

■ Add a little extra oil to the pan, then add the onions and fry for 5 minutes until just beginning to soften and lightly brown. Stir in the sugar and fry for a further 5 minutes until a deep brown, being careful not to have the heat too high so that you don't burn the onions.

■ Stir in the stock, tomato purée and mustard. Mix the cornflour with 2 teaspoons of cold water in a small bowl, stir into the onions and season with salt and pepper. Bring to the boil stirring.

■ Arrange the sausages in a single layer in the slow cooker pot, pour over the onion mix and cover with the lid. Cook on High for 4–5 hours until the sausages are completely cooked through.

■ Peel the potatoes and cut into small evenly-sized pieces. Boil in salted water until soft, about 25 minutes, and mash until smooth. Cook the green beans in a pan of salted water for 5 minutes. Serve with the sausages and gravy.

MAKE IT MEATY

For pork sausages with onion gravy, grill 8 pork sausages, instead of the Quorn ones, until browned but not cooked through. Make the onion gravy as for the main recipe, then add the sausages and gravy to the slow cooker pot and cook as for the main recipe for 5–6 hours until the sausages are cooked through.

SERVES 4

Preparation time 15 minutes
Cooking temperature Low and High
Cooking time 5½–7½ hours

INGREDIENTS

1	1 red pepper, cored, deseeded and diced
2	400 g (13 oz) can chopped tomatoes
3	2 sprigs of thyme
4	400 g (13 oz) pack frozen seafood (prawns, mussels, squid), thawed
5	300 g (10 oz) tagliatelle

STORECUPBOARD

1 onion, finely chopped; 2 garlic cloves, finely chopped; 150 ml (¼ pint) fish stock; 1 tablespoon olive oil; salt and black pepper

Baked Seafood Tagliatelle

■ Preheat the slow cooker if necessary, see manufacturer's instructions. Put the onion, red pepper, garlic and tomatoes into the slow cooker pot, then add the stock, thyme, oil and a little salt and pepper.

■ Cover with the lid and cook on Low for 5–7 hours. Rinse the seafood with cold water, drain and then stir into the slow cooker pot. Replace the lid and cook on High for 30 minutes or until piping hot.

■ When almost ready to serve, bring a large saucepan of water to the boil, add the pasta and cook for 8–10 minutes or until just tender. Drain and spoon into shallow bowls and top with the seafood sauce.

USE SALMON INSTEAD

For baked salmon with pesto, omit the seafood and drain a 400 g (13 oz) can red salmon, remove the skin and bones and break the fish into large flakes. Put the onion, red pepper and garlic into the slow cooker pot. Heat the tomatoes and stock in a small saucepan or the microwave, then add to the pot with 2 teaspoons pesto and the oil, omitting the thyme. Mix in the salmon and continue as for the main recipe.

Preparation time 20 minutes
Cooking temperature Low
Cooking time 8–10 hours

INGREDIENTS

1	750 g (1½ lb) lean stewing beef, cubed
2	330 ml (11 fl oz) can ginger beer
3	6 teaspoons tamarind paste
4	1 teaspoon ground mixed spice
5	broccoli florets, to serve

STORECUPBOARD

2 tablespoons sunflower oil; 1 onion, chopped;
2 garlic cloves, finely chopped; 2 tablespoons plain
flour; 1 tablespoon dark muscovado sugar; salt and
black pepper

Tamarind Beef with Ginger Beer

■ Preheat the slow cooker if necessary,
see manufacturer's instructions. Heat the
oil in a large frying pan, add the beef a few
pieces at a time, then add the onion and fry
over a medium heat, stirring, until the meat
is evenly browned.

■ Stir in the garlic and flour. Gradually mix
in the ginger beer, then stir in the tamarind
paste and spice, sugar and a little salt and
pepper and bring to the boil, stirring.

■ Transfer to the slow cooker pot and
press the beef below the surface of the
liquid. Cover with the lid and cook on Low
for 8–10 hours or until the meat is cooked
through and tender.

■ Stir the beef, then ladle into bowls and
top with garlic and coriander croutes (see
right) and serve with steamed broccoli.

ADD CROUTES

For ginger & coriander croutes, beat a 2 cm (¾ inch) piece peeled and grated root ginger with 2 finely chopped garlic cloves and 50 g (2 oz) butter, stir in ½ mild, deseeded, finely chopped red chilli, 3 tablespoons chopped coriander leaves and a little salt and pepper. Toast 8 slices of French bread on both sides and spread with the butter while hot. Arrange the croutes on top of the casserole and serve immediately.

SERVES 4

Preparation time 25 minutes
Cooking temperature Low
Cooking time 1¾–2¼ hours

INGREDIENTS

1 100 g (3½ oz) butter

2 500 g (1 lb) piece of thick end salmon fillet, no longer than 18 cm (7 inches)

3 1 bay leaf

4 200 ml (7 fl oz) dry white wine

5 3 tablespoons finely chopped chives, plus extra to garnish

STORECUPBOARD

1 large onion, thinly sliced; 1 lemon, sliced; 150 ml (¼ pint) fish stock; salt and black pepper; lemon slices, to garnish

Poached Salmon with Beurre Blanc

■ Preheat the slow cooker if necessary, see manufacturer's instructions. Brush inside the slow cooker pot with a little butter. Fold a large piece of kitchen foil into 3, then place it at the bottom of the pot with the ends sticking up to use as a strap. Arrange the onion slices and half the lemon slices over the foil. Place the salmon, flesh side up, on top. Season with salt and pepper, add the bay leaf and remaining lemon.

■ Pour the wine and stock into a saucepan, bring to the boil, then pour over the salmon. Fit the cooker lid, then cook on Low for 1¾–2¼ hours until the fish is opaque and flakes easily when pressed in the centre with a knife.

■ Lift the salmon carefully out of the pot using the foil strap, draining off as much

liquid as possible. Transfer to a serving plate, discard the bay leaf, lemon and onion, and keep warm. Strain the cooking liquid into a saucepan and boil rapidly for 4–5 minutes, until reduced to about 4 tablespoons.

■ Reduce the heat and gradually whisk in small pieces of the remaining butter, little by little, until the sauce thickens and becomes creamy. (Don't be tempted to hurry making the sauce either by adding the butter in one go or by increasing the heat to the sauce, or you may find that it separates.) Stir in the chopped chives and adjust the seasoning if needed.

■ Cut the salmon into 4 portions, discard the skin and transfer to individual plates. Spoon a little of the sauce around the fish. Garnish with lemon slices and chives.

Preparation time 15 minutes
Cooking temperature High and Low
Cooking time 6–7 hours

INGREDIENTS

1 6 boneless, skinless chicken thighs, about 500 g (1 lb) in total, cubed

2 375 g (12 oz) sweet potatoes, cut into 2 cm (¾ inch) cubes

3 425 g (14 oz) jar balti curry sauce

4 chopped coriander, to garnish (optional)

5 2 naan breads

STORECUPBOARD

1 onion, sliced; 2 garlic cloves, finely chopped

Chicken & Sweet Potato Balti

■ Preheat the slow cooker if necessary, see manufacturer's instructions. Arrange the chicken, onion and sweet potatoes in the base of the slow cooker pot in an even layer. Sprinkle with the garlic.

■ Bring the curry sauce just to the boil in a small saucepan or the microwave. Pour into the slow cooker pot in an even layer. Cover with the lid and cook on High for 30 minutes. Reduce the heat and cook on Low for 5½–6½ hours, or set to auto for 6–7 hours, until the chicken is cooked through and the sauce piping hot.

■ Stir well, then sprinkle with roughly chopped coriander, if liked. Spoon into bowls and serve with warmed naan bread.

TRY A DIFFERENT SPICY HEAT

For harissa baked chicken, prepare the chicken and vegetables but replace the curry sauce with 400 g (13 oz) can chopped tomatoes and 2 teaspoons harissa paste. Continue as for the main recipe.

Preparation time 15 minutes
Cooking temperature High
Cooking time 3–4 hours

INGREDIENTS

1 200 g (7 oz) red lentils, rinsed with cold water, drained

2 2 teaspoons medium curry powder

3 1 medium cauliflower, cut into small florets, 400 g (13 oz) prepared weight

4 1 teaspoon turmeric

5 1 teaspoon garam masala

STORECUPBOARD

750 ml (1¼ pints) boiling water; ½ teaspoon salt; black pepper; 1 onion, halved, thinly sliced; 1 tablespoon sunflower oil

Easy Cauliflower Dahl

■ Preheat the slow cooker if necessary, see manufacturer's instructions. Add the lentils, boiling water and curry powder to the slow cooker pot, then stir in the salt and pepper.

■ Cover with the lid and cook on High for 3–4 hours or until the lentils are soft.

■ When almost ready to serve, add the cauliflower to a large saucepan, add 6 tablespoons of water, then cover and cook over medium heat for 5 minutes until the cauliflower is almost cooked. Drain off any excess water, then add the onion and a little oil, increase the heat and fry for 2–3 minutes.

■ Sprinkle over the garam masala and turmeric and fry, stirring for 4–5 minutes until the cauliflower and onion is golden brown. Season with salt and pepper.

■ Stir the lentil dahl, spoon into shallow bowls, then spoon the cauliflower mix on top.

SERVES 4

Preparation time 30 minutes
Cooking temperature High and Low
Cooking time 6–8 hours

INGREDIENTS

1 | 8 boneless, skinless chicken thighs, about 700 g (1 lb 6 oz) in total, each cut into 3 or 4 pieces

2 | 2–3 sprigs of oregano

3 | 300 g (10 oz) macaroni or orzo pasta

4 | 2 eggs plus 2 egg yolks

5 | 4 tablespoons chopped parsley, plus extra to garnish (optional)

STORECUPBOARD

1 onion, thinly sliced; 450 ml (¾ pint) boiling chicken stock; grated rind and juice of 1 lemon; salt and black pepper

Chicken Avgolemono

■ Preheat the slow cooker if necessary, see manufacturer's instructions. Put the chicken, onion and oregano into the slow cooker pot. Mix the stock, lemon rind and juice and salt and pepper, then pour over the chicken.

■ Cover with the lid and cook on High for 30 minutes. Reduce the heat and cook on Low for 5½–7½ hours, or set to auto for 6–8 hours, until the chicken is cooked through and tender. When almost ready to serve, bring a large saucepan of water to the boil, add the pasta and cook for 9–10 minutes or until just tender.

■ Meanwhile, drain the stock from the slow cooker pot into a second large saucepan and boil for 5 minutes until reduced by one-third or to about 200 ml (7 fl oz).

Whisk the eggs and egg yolks in a bowl, then gradually whisk in 2 ladlefuls of stock until smooth. Pour into the reduced stock, then whisk over a gentle heat until the sauce has thickened slightly. Stir in the parsley.

■ Pour the sauce over the chicken. Spoon the pasta into shallow bowls and top with the chicken. Sprinkle with extra chopped parsley.

MAKE A FISH VERSION

For salmon avgolemono, lower a
500 g (1 lb) thick piece of salmon
into the slow cooker pot over a
triple thickness strip of foil, add 6
thinly sliced spring onions and the
oregano. Pour over 350 ml (12 fl oz)
boiling fish stock mixed with the
lemon rind and juice and salt and
pepper. Cover and cook on Low for
2½–3 hours or until the fish flakes
easily when pressed in the centre
with a knife. Cook the pasta and
make the sauce as for the main
recipe, omitting the parsley. Lift the
salmon out with the foil, skin and
flake into large chunks, then toss
with the sauce and pasta.

SERVES 4

Preparation time 5 minutes
Cooking temperature High
Cooking time 7–8 hours

INGREDIENTS

1 1–1.2 kg (2–2 lb 7 oz) half lamb shoulder on the bone

2 3 sprigs of rosemary

3 2 tablespoons redcurrant jelly

4 250 ml (8 fl oz) red wine

STORECUPBOARD

1 red onion, cut into wedges; 250 ml (8 fl oz) lamb stock; salt and black pepper

Pot-roasted Lamb with Rosemary

■ Preheat the slow cooker if necessary, see manufacturer's instructions. Put the lamb into the slow cooker pot, add the rosemary on top and tuck the onion wedges around the sides of the joint.

■ Spoon the redcurrant jelly into a small saucepan and add the wine, stock and a little salt and pepper. Bring to the boil, stirring so that the jelly melts, then pour over the lamb. Cover with the lid and cook on High for 7–8 hours or until a knife goes into the centre of the lamb easily and the meat is almost falling off the bone.

■ Lift the joint out of the slow cooker pot and put it on to a serving plate with the onions. Discard the rosemary sprigs and pour the wine and stock mixture into a jug to serve as gravy. Carve the lamb on

to plates and serve with steamed green vegetables and rosemary new potatoes (see right).

A VEGETABLE ACCOMPANIMENT

For green vegetables and rosemary new potatoes, bring a pan of water to the boil, add 500 g (1 lb) baby new potatoes and cook for 15 minutes. Add 200 g (7 oz) mixed green vegetables, thickly sliced, for the last 5 minutes. Drain and then stir in 1 tablespoon finely chopped rosemary and a little salt and pepper.

SERVES 4

Preparation time 20 minutes
Cooking temperature Low
Cooking time 6¼–8¼ hours

INGREDIENTS

1	175 g (6 oz) pearl barley
2	500 g (1 lb) butternut squash, peeled, deseeded and cut into 2 cm (¾ inch) pieces
3	125 g (4 oz) baby spinach, washed and well drained
4	100 g (3½ oz) butter, at room temperature
5	100 g (3½ oz) blue cheese (rind removed)

STORECUPBOARD

1 onion, finely chopped; 2 garlic cloves, finely chopped; 1 litre (1¾ pints) boiling vegetable stock; 1 garlic clove, finely chopped; salt and black pepper

Barley Risotto with Blue Cheese

■ Preheat the slow cooker if necessary, see manufacturer's instructions. Put the pearl barley, onion, garlic and butternut squash into the slow cooker pot. Add the stock and a little salt and pepper. Cover with the lid and cook on Low for 6–8 hours or until the barley and squash are tender.

■ Meanwhile, make the blue cheese butter. Put the butter on a plate, crumble the cheese on top, add the garlic and mash it all together with a fork. Spoon the butter into a line on a piece of nonstick baking paper, then wrap it in paper and roll it backwards and forwards to make a neat sausage shape. Chill in the refrigerator until required.

■ When almost ready to serve, stir the risotto, slice half the blue cheese butter and add to the slow cooker pot. Mix together until just beginning to melt, then add the spinach. Replace the lid and cook, still on Low, for 15 minutes or until the spinach has just wilted. Ladle into shallow bowls and top with slices of the remaining butter.

MAKE IT CREAMY

For barley risotto with garlic &
coriander cream, make the risotto
as for the main recipe, replacing
the squash with 500 g (1 lb) sweet
potato and adding 150 g (5 oz)
sliced cup mushrooms with the
stock. Cook as for the main recipe,
omitting spinach and blue cheese
butter. Mix together 200 g (7 oz)
crème fraîche, 1 finely chopped
garlic clove and 3 chopped spring
onions. Ladle into bowls and top
with spoonfuls of the cream.

SERVES 4

Preparation time 15 minutes
Cooking temperature High
Cooking time 1½–2 hours

INGREDIENTS

1	1 large carrot, cut into matchsticks
2	1 large celery stick, thinly sliced
3	6 small herrings, gutted, filleted and rinsed with cold water
4	2 stems of tarragon plus tarragon sprigs, to garnish
5	1 bay leaf

STORECUPBOARD

1 large red onion, thinly sliced; 150 ml (¼ pint) cider vinegar; 25 g (1 oz) caster sugar; 600 ml (1 pint) boiling water; ½ teaspoon coloured peppercorns; salt

Hot Soused Herrings

■ Preheat the slow cooker if necessary, see manufacturer's instructions. Put half the onion, carrot and celery in the base of the slow cooker pot. Arrange the herring fillets on top, then cover with the remaining vegetables.

■ Add the tarragon, bay leaf, vinegar and sugar, then pour over the boiling water. Add the peppercorns and a little salt. Cover with the lid and cook on High for 1½–2 hours.

■ Spoon the fish, vegetables and a little of the cooking liquid into shallow bowls, halving the fish fillets if liked. Garnish with tarragon sprigs.

TRY A SWEDISH VARIATION
For Swedish baked herrings, make
as for the main recipe, adding
2 sprigs dill instead of tarragon and
increasing the sugar to 50 g (2 oz).
Leave to cool once cooked and
serve with 8 tablespoons soured
cream mixed with 1 teaspoon hot
horseradish.

SERVES 4

Preparation time 20 minutes
Cooking temperature Low
Cooking time 8½–9½ hours

INGREDIENTS

1. 6 skinless, boneless chicken thighs, 625 g (1¼ lb), halved

2. 1 fennel bulb, 250 g (8 oz) in total, halved, core cut away, then sliced, any green fronds reserved

3. 2 leeks, 300 g (10 oz) in total, thinly sliced, white and green slices kept separate

4. ½ orange, grated rind and juice

5. 3 tablespoons fresh chopped parsley to garnish

STORECUPBOARD

1 tablespoon sunflower oil; 350 ml (12 fl oz) chicken stock; 2 teaspoons cornflour; salt and black pepper

Tangy Chicken, Fennel & Leek Braise

■ Preheat the slow cooker if necessary, see manufacturer's instructions. Heat the oil in a large frying pan, then add the chicken and brown on both sides. Lift out with a draining spoon and put on a plate.

■ Add the white fennel and white leeks to the frying pan and cook for 2–3 minutes until just softened. Stir in the stock, orange rind and juice. Mix the cornflour to a smooth paste with 2 teaspoons cold water, then stir into the pan. Season with salt and pepper and bring to the boil stirring.

■ Spoon the fennel mix into the slow cooker, add the chicken pieces in a single layer and press beneath the surface of the liquid. Cover with the lid and cook on Low for 8–9 hours until the chicken is cooked with no hint of pink juices.

■ Add the reserved green leek slices and any green fennel fronds to the slow cooker, mix into the sauce, then cover with the lid and cook for 30 minutes. Serve garnished with chopped parsley.

MAKE IT MUSTARDY

For braised mustard chicken &
leeks, omit the fennel and orange
and add 75 g (3 oz) diced lean back
bacon when frying the white sliced
leeks. Stir in the stock, 1 teaspoon
Dijon mustard, then the cornflour
and seasoning. Cook as for the main
recipe and finish with the green
sliced leeks for the last 30 minutes.
Garnish with parsley.

SERVES 4

Preparation time 25 minutes
Cooking temperature Low
Cooking time 8–10 hours

INGREDIENTS

1	8 chilli or spicy sausages
2	150 g (5 oz) cup mushrooms, sliced
3	400 g (13 oz) can chopped tomatoes
4	250 g (8 oz) tagliatelle
5	basil leaves

STORECUPBOARD

1 tablespoon sunflower oil; 1 onion, chopped;
2 garlic cloves, finely chopped; 150 ml (¼ pint)
beef stock; salt and black pepper

Sausage Tagliatelle

■ Preheat the slow cooker if necessary, see manufacturer's instructions. Heat the oil in a large frying pan, add the sausages and fry, turning until browned but not cooked through. Transfer to the slow cooker pot with tongs.

■ Drain off the excess fat from the pan to leave 2 teaspoons, then add the onion and fry until softened. Mix in the mushrooms and garlic and fry for 1–2 minutes.

■ Stir in the chopped tomatoes, stock and a little salt and pepper and bring to the boil, stirring. Pour the mixture over the sausages, cover with the lid and cook on Low for 8–10 hours or until cooked through.

■ When almost ready to serve, bring a large saucepan of water to the boil, add the tagliatelle and cook for 7–8 minutes or until just tender, then drain. Lift the sausages out of the slow cooker pot and slice thickly, then return to the pot with the pasta and mix together. Sprinkle with torn basil leaves.

FOR A SPANISH FLAVOUR

For chicken & chorizo tagliatelle, omit the sausages and fry 500 g (1 lb) diced boneless chicken thighs in 1 tablespoon olive oil until golden. Drain and transfer to the slow cooker pot. Continue as for the main recipe, omitting the basil and adding 100 g (3½ oz) diced chorizo sausage to the frying pan with the onions and replacing the beef stock with 150 ml (¼ pint) chicken stock.

SERVES 3-4

Preparation time 20 minutes
Cooking temperature High
Cooking time 3-4 hours

INGREDIENTS

1 **3 different coloured peppers, cored, deseeded and diced**

2 **400 g (13 oz) can chopped tomatoes**

3 **2 sprigs of basil plus leaves, to garnish**

4 **500 g (1 lb) pack chilled gnocchi**

5 **freshly grated Parmesan cheese, to serve**

STORECUPBOARD

2 tablespoons olive oil; 1 onion, chopped; 2 garlic cloves, finely chopped; 1 tablespoon plain flour; 1 teaspoon caster sugar; 150 ml (¼ pint) vegetable stock; salt and black pepper

Pepperonata

■ Preheat the slow cooker if necessary, see manufacturer's instructions. Heat the oil in a large frying pan, add the onion and fry, stirring frequently, until softened. Add the peppers and garlic and fry for a further 1-2 minutes.

■ Stir in the flour, mix in the tomatoes, then add the sugar, the basil, torn into pieces, stock and a little salt and pepper. Bring to the boil, then pour into the slow cooker pot. Cover with the lid and cook on High for 3-4 hours or until the peppers are tender.

■ When almost ready to serve, bring a large saucepan of water to the boil, add the gnocchi and cook for 2-3 minutes or until they float to the surface and are piping hot. Drain and gently stir into the pepperonata

in the slow cooker pot. Spoon into shallow bowls and sprinkle with torn basil leaves and grated Parmesan.

MAKE A BEANY STEW

For pepperonata & white bean stew, add a 410 g (13½ oz) can drained haricot beans with the tomatoes. Continue as for the main recipe, omitting the gnocchi.

FAMILY
FAVOURITES

Preparation time 20 minutes
Cooking temperature High
Cooking time 2½–3 hours

INGREDIENTS

1	250 g (8 oz) rigatoni
2	250 g (8 oz) cup mushrooms, sliced
3	650 g (21 oz) tinned tomatoes, cut into chunks
4	1 tablespoon tomato purée
5	freshly grated Parmesan cheese, to serve

STORECUPBOARD

3 tablespoons olive oil; 1 onion, sliced; 2–3 garlic cloves, finely chopped; 200 ml (7 fl oz) vegetable stock; salt and black pepper

Mushroom & Tomato Rigatoni

■ Preheat the slow cooker if necessary, see manufacturer's instructions. Put the pasta into a large bowl, cover with boiling water and leave to stand for 10 minutes while preparing the rest of the dish.

■ Heat 1 tablespoon of the oil in a large frying pan, add the onion and fry until softened. Stir in the remaining oil, garlic and mushrooms and fry, stirring, until the mushrooms are just beginning to brown.

■ Stir in the tomatoes, stock and tomato purée. Add a little salt and pepper and bring to the boil.

■ Drain the pasta and put it in the slow cooker pot, pour over the hot mushroom mixture and spread into an even layer. Cover with the lid and cook on Low for 2½–3 hours or until the pasta is just tender.

■ Spoon into shallow bowls and sprinkle with grated Parmesan.

SERVES 4

Preparation time 20 minutes
Cooking temperature High
Cooking time 5–6 hours

INGREDIENTS

1	**875 g (1¾ lb) half lower lamb leg joint on the bone**
2	**1 leek, 175 g (6 oz), thickly sliced**
3	**1 tablespoon redcurrant jelly**
4	**15 g (½ oz) fresh mint, leaves torn from stems and chopped, plus extra to serve**
5	**700 g (27 oz) mixed vegetables (celeriac, swede and baby Chantanay carrots) peeled, cut into 2 cm (¾ inch) cubes**

STORECUPBOARD

1½ tablespoons sunflower oil; salt and black pepper; 2 teaspoons plain flour; 450 ml (¾ pint) lamb stock

Winter Warming Lamb Pot Roast

■ Preheat the slow cooker if necessary, see manufacturer's instructions. Heat a tablespoon of the oil in a large frying pan and add the lamb sprinkled with a little salt and pepper. Fry for 5–10 minutes, turning until browned on all sides. Lift out and transfer to the slow cooker pot.

■ Add the white parts of the sliced leeks to the frying pan with a little extra oil, cook for 2–3 minutes, then sprinkle the flour over and mix together. Reserve the green sliced leeks for later.

■ Pour in the stock, add the redcurrant jelly and chopped mint, then bring to the boil stirring. Spoon the celeriac, swede and carrots around the lamb, then pour over the fried leeks and stock. Cover and cook on High for 5–6 hours until the lamb is beginning to fall of the bone and the vegetables are tender. Add the green leek slices for the last 15 minutes of cooking.

■ Lift the lamb out of the slow cooker pot and break into pieces, add to shallow bowls with spoonfuls of the hot vegetables and the minty stock. If you would prefer the stock to be thicker, drain into a saucepan and boil rapidly on the hob to reduce down by half. Sprinkle with extra small mint leaves and serve.

Preparation time 15 minutes
Cooking temperature High
Cooking time 4–5 hours

INGREDIENTS

1	**800 g (26 oz) fresh tomatoes, (no need to peel) diced**
2	**small handful fresh basil, torn into pieces, plus extra to serve**
3	**2 large aubergines (about 500 gg/1 lb), sliced**
4	**75 g (3 oz) mature white cheese cheese, grated**
5	**2 tablespoons finely grated Parmesan**

STORECUPBOARD

1 tablespoon olive oil; 1 onion, chopped; 2 garlic
cloves, finely chopped; 2 teaspoons granulated
sugar; 2 teaspoons cornflour; salt and black
pepper

Aubergine Parmigiana

■ Preheat the slow cooker if necessary,
see manufacturer's instructions. Heat the
oil in a large frying pan, add the onion and
fry for 4–5 minutes until just beginning to
soften and colour.

■ Stir in the garlic and tomatoes, then mix
in the basil and sugar. Mix the cornflour to
a paste with 2 teaspoons cold water, stir
into the sauce with salt and pepper. Bring
to the boil stirring.

■ Spoon a little of the tomato sauce over
the base of the slow cooker pot, arrange
one third of the aubergines overlapping
on top, spoon over a thin layer of the
sauce and add a little grated white cheese.
Repeat to make three aubergine layers,
finishing with a generous layer of the
tomato sauce and grated cheese.

■ Cover with the lid and cook on High for
4–5 hours until the aubergines are soft.
Sprinkle with the Parmesan and extra
basil leaves.

TRY IT WITH MUSHROOMS

For mushroom parmigiana, make up the tomato sauce, then layer in the slow cooker pot with 8 large flat field mushrooms instead of the aubergines, in two layers. Bake and serve as for the main recipe.

SERVES 4

Preparation time 15 minutes
Cooking temperature Low
Cooking time 1½–2 hours

INGREDIENTS

1	2 x 410 g (13½ oz) cans cannellini beans, drained
2	1 teaspoon wholegrain mustard
3	4 smoked cod loins, about 625 g (1¼ lb) in total
4	4 tablespoons crème fraîche
5	small bunch of parsley, watercress or rocket leaves, roughly chopped

STORECUPBOARD

1 onion, thinly sliced; 400 ml (14 fl oz) boiling fish stock; grated rind and juice of 1 lemon; salt and black pepper

Smoked Cod with Bean Mash

■ Preheat the slow cooker if necessary, see manufacturer's instructions. Put the beans into the slow cooker pot with the onion slices. Mix the fish stock with the mustard, lemon rind and juice and a little salt and pepper, then pour into the pot.

■ Arrange the fish on top and sprinkle with a little extra pepper. Cover with the lid and cook on Low for 1½–2 hours or until the fish flakes easily when pressed in the centre with a knife.

■ Lift out the fish with a fish slice and transfer to a plate. Pour off nearly all the cooking liquid, then mash the beans roughly. Stir in the crème fraîche and the parsley, watercress or rocket. Taste and adjust the seasoning, if needed. Spoon the mash on to plates and top with the fish.

TRY IT WITH SALMON AND BASIL

For baked salmon with basil bean mash, add the beans to the slow cooker pot with the ingredients as for the main recipe, omitting the mustard. Arrange 4 x 150 g (5 oz) salmon steaks on top, season and cook as for the main recipe. Mash the beans with the crème fraîche, a tablespoon of finely chopped basil and green spring onions and serve with the fish.

SERVES 4–5

Preparation time 25 minutes
Cooking temperature High
Cooking time 5–6 hours

INGREDIENTS

1   **1.5 kg (3 lb) whole chicken**

2   **500 ml (17 fl oz) dry cider**

3   **3 carrots, cut into chunks**

4   **3 celery sticks, thickly sliced**

5   **20 g (¾ oz) tarragon**

STORECUPBOARD

2 tablespoons olive oil; 1 large onion, cut into 6 wedges; 2 teaspoons caster sugar; 900 ml (1½ pints) hot chicken stock; 1 lemon, cut into 6 wedges; 1 tablespoon cornflour; salt and pepper

Pot-roasted Chicken with Lemon

■ Preheat the slow cooker if necessary, see manufacturer's instructions. Heat the oil in a large frying pan, add the chicken, breast side down, and fry for 10 minutes, turning the chicken until browned all over.

■ Put the chicken, breast side down, in the slow cooker pot. Fry the onion wedges in the remaining oil in the pan until lightly browned. Add the cider and sugar and season with salt and pepper. Bring to the boil, then pour over the chicken. Add the hot stock, then the vegetables, lemon wedges and 3 sprigs of the tarragon, making sure that the chicken and all the vegetables are well below the level of the stock so that they cook evenly and thoroughly.

■ Cover with the lid and cook on High for 5–6 hours or until the chicken is thoroughly cooked and the meat juices run clear when the thickest parts of the leg and breast are pierced with a sharp knife. Turn the chicken after 4 hours, if liked.

■ Lift the chicken out of the stock, drain well and transfer to a large serving plate. Remove the vegetables with a slotted spoon and arrange them around the chicken. Measure 600 ml (1 pint) of the hot cooking stock from the slow cooker pot into a jug. Reserve a few sprigs of tarragon to garnish, chop the remainder and whisk into the jug with the cornflour to make a gravy. Adjust the seasoning to taste. Carve the chicken in the usual way and serve with the gravy and vegetables. Garnish with the reserved tarragon.

SERVES 4

Preparation time 10 minutes
Cooking temperature High
Cooking time 3–4 hours

INGREDIENTS

1	**750 g (1½ lb) plum tomatoes, halved**
2	**4 tablespoons white wine**
3	**375 g (12 oz) spaghetti**
4	**basil leaves, to garnish**
5	**freshly grated or shaved Parmesan cheese, to serve**

STORECUPBOARD

1 tablespoon olive oil, for greasing; 4 teaspoons good balsamic vinegar; salt and black pepper

Balsamic Tomatoes with Spaghetti

■ Preheat the slow cooker if necessary, see manufacturer's instructions. Brush the oil over the base of the slow cooker pot, add the tomatoes, cut side down, drizzle over the wine and vinegar and add a little salt and pepper. Cover with the lid and cook on High for 3–4 hours or until the tomatoes are tender.

■ When almost ready to serve, bring a large saucepan of water to the boil, add the pasta and cook for 6–7 minutes or until tender. Drain and mix into the sauce. Spoon the pasta into bowls and sprinkle with basil leaves and grated or shaved Parmesan.

FOR A PESTO TWIST

For pesto baked tomatoes, oil the base of the slow cooker pot as for the main recipe, sprinkling with 2 finely chopped garlic cloves before adding the tomatoes. Drizzle with 1 tablespoon pesto sauce, omitting the vinegar and wine. Cook and serve as for the main recipe.

Preparation time 20 minutes
Cooking temperature Low and High
Cooking time 8¼–10½ hours

INGREDIENTS

1 625 g (1¼ lb) or 7, boneless, skinless chicken thighs, each cut into 3 pieces

2 2 small carrots or 125 g (4 oz), peeled, cut into small dice

3 15 g (½ oz) bunch basil leaves, torn into pieces, plus extra tiny leaves to garnish

4 100 g (3½ oz) frozen peas, just defrosted

5 350 g (12 oz) tenderstem broccoli, stems cut into 3 or 4 pieces

STORECUPBOARD

1½ tablespoons sunflower oil; 1 onion, chopped; 2 teaspoons plain flour; 350 ml (12 fl oz) chicken stock; salt and black pepper

Chicken & Pesto Stew Pots

■ Preheat the slow cooker if necessary, see manufacturer's instructions. Heat a tablespoon of the oil in a large frying pan, then add the chicken a few pieces at a time until all the pieces are in the pan. Fry for 5 minutes, until browned on both sides. Lift out of the pan with a draining spoon and put into the slow cooker pot.

■ Add a little more oil if needed, then fry the onion for 4–5 minutes, until just beginning to soften. Stir in the carrots and flour, then mix in the stock and bring to the boil. Stir in the basil and a little salt and pepper, then pour over the chicken.

■ Cover with the lid and cook on Low for 8–10 hours until the chicken is tender and there are no pink juices when a piece is pierced. Increase the heat to High and add the peas and broccoli. Recover and cook for 15–30 minutes until tender, then ladle into shallow bowls and garnish with extra basil leaves.

TRY CHICKEN WITH GARLIC

For chunky chicken with 30 garlic cloves, leave the chicken thighs whole, brown as for the main recipe, then add 250 g (8 oz) peeled shallots, halved if large in place of the onion and carrot. Cook as for the main recipe, then add the flour, chicken stock and 3 stems of fresh thyme instead of basil. Separate 2–3 garlic bulbs and add 30 unpeeled cloves to the chicken with 2 teaspoons Dijon mustard. Cook on Low for 8–10 hours and serve sprinkled with chopped parsley rather than the green vegetables.

SERVES 4

Preparation time 15 minutes
Cooking temperature Low
Cooking time 6–8 hours

INGREDIENTS

1	8 'gourmet' flavoured sausages, such as Sicilian or Toulouse
2	1 tablespoon sun-dried or ordinary tomato purée
3	4 large Yorkshire puddings
4	3 large carrots
5	1 head broccoli

STORECUPBOARD

1 tablespoon sunflower oil; 2 red onions, halved and thinly sliced; 2 teaspoons light muscovado sugar; 2 tablespoons plain flour; 450 ml (¾ pint) beef stock; salt and black pepper

Sausages with Yorkshire Pudding

■ Preheat the slow cooker if necessary, see manufacturer's instructions. Heat the oil in a frying pan, add the sausages and fry over a high heat for 5 minutes, turning until browned on all sides but not cooked through. Drain and transfer to the slow cooker pot.

■ Add the onions to the frying pan and fry over a medium heat for 5 minutes or until softened. Add the sugar and fry, stirring, for 5 more minutes or until the onion slices are caramelized around the edges.

■ Stir in the flour, then gradually mix in the stock. Add the tomato purée and some salt and pepper and bring to the boil, still stirring. Pour over the sausages. Cover with the lid and cook on Low for 6–8 hours or until the sausages are tender.

■ Serve spooned into reheated ready-made large Yorkshire puddings accompanied with the steamed carrots and broccoli.

TRY A BEER GRAVY

For sausages with beery onion gravy, fry 8 large traditional herb sausages until browned. Fry 2 sliced white onions until softened, and omit the sugar. Stir in plain flour, then mix in 150 ml (¼ pint) stout or brown beer and reduce the beef stock to 300 ml (½ pint). Replace the tomato purée with 1 tablespoon wholegrain mustard and 2 tablespoons Worcestershire sauce. Season and bring to the boil. Cook in the slow cooker for 6–8 hours.

Preparation time 10 minutes
Cooking temperature Low
Cooking time 5¼–6¼ hours

INGREDIENTS

1 | 540 g (1 lb 3 oz) can balti curry sauce

2 | 1 large cauliflower, trimmed and cut into large pieces, about 750 g (1½ lb) prepared weight

3 | 410 g (13½ oz) can green lentils, drained

4 | 150 g (5 oz) spinach, washed and torn into pieces

5 | naan bread to serve

STORECUPBOARD

1 tablespoon sunflower oil; 1 onion, chopped

Cauliflower & Spinach Balti

■ Preheat the slow cooker if necessary, see manufacturer's instructions. Heat the oil in a large frying pan, add the onion and fry, stirring, for 5 minutes or until softened. Add the curry sauce and bring to the boil.

■ Put the cauliflower and lentils into the slow cooker pot, then pour over the hot sauce. Cover with the lid and cook on Low for 5–6 hours or until the cauliflower is tender.

■ Stir the cauliflower and lentil mixture and sprinkle the spinach on top. Replace the lid and cook, still on Low, for 10–15 minutes or until the spinach has just wilted. Spoon into bowls and serve with warm naan bread.

USE DIFFERENT VEGETABLES

For mushroom & sweet potato balti, make the sauce as for the main recipe. Replace the cauliflower with 375 g (12 oz) quartered cup mushrooms and 375 g (12 oz) diced sweet potatoes and put into the slow cooker pot omitting the lentils. Pour over the sauce, cover with the lid and cook on Low for 6 7 hours or until the sweet potatoes are tender. Add the spinach and cook and serve as for the main recipe.

SERVES 4

Preparation time 40 minutes
Cooking temperature High
Cooking time 5-6 hours

INGREDIENTS

1   25 g (1 oz) butter, plus extra for greasing

2   100 g (3½ oz) cup mushrooms, sliced

3   1 teaspoon Dijon mustard

4   700 g (1 lb 6 oz) rump steak, thinly sliced and any fat discarded

5   150 g (5 oz) shredded suet

STORECUPBOARD

1 tablespoon sunflower oil; 2 large onions, roughly chopped; 2 teaspoons caster sugar; 300 g (10 oz) plus 1 tablespoon self-raising flour; 150 ml (¼ pint) hot beef stock; salt and black pepper; 200 ml (7 fl oz) water

Steak & Mushroom Pudding

■ Preheat the slow cooker if necessary, see manufacturer's instructions. Heat the butter and oil in a frying pan, add the onions and fry for 5 minutes or until softened. Sprinkle the sugar over the onions and fry for 5 more minutes or until browned. Add the mushrooms and fry for 2-3 minutes. Stir in the 1 tablespoon of flour.

■ Mix together the stock, mustard and salt and pepper in a jug.

■ Make the suet pastry. Mix the flour, salt and suet well in a bowl. Gradually stir in water to make a soft, not sticky, dough. Knead lightly, then, on a floured surface, roll out a circle 33 cm (13 inches) across. Cut out and reserve a quarter segment.

■ Press the dough into a 1.5 litre (2½ pint) buttered basin, butting the edges together.

■ Layer the fried onions, mushrooms and sliced steak in the basin. Pour the stock over the top. Pat the reserved pastry into a round the same size as the top of the basin. Fold the top edges of the pastry in the basin over the filling, brush with a little water and cover with the pastry lid.

■ Cover the pudding with a domed circle of buttered foil leaving room for it to rise. Tie with string. Stand the basin in the slow cooker pot on top of an upturned saucer. Pour in boiling water to come halfway up the sides of the basin. Cover with the lid and cook on High for 5-6 hours.

■ Remove the basin from the slow cooker using a tea towel and remove the string and foil. The pastry should have risen and feel dry to the touch.

Preparation time 20 minutes
Cooking temperature High
Cooking time 3-4 hours

INGREDIENTS

1   **2 large red peppers, each 150 g (5 oz), halved lengthways leaving the stalks on, cored and deseeded**

2   **50 g (2 oz) chorizo sausage, cut into small dice**

3   **200 g (7 oz) cherry tomatoes, halved**

4   **few sprigs fresh basil, plus extra to garnish**

5   **4 pinches smoked hot paprika**

STORECUPBOARD

2 spring onions, trimmed, thinly sliced; 1-2 garlic cloves, finely chopped; 1 tablespoon balsamic vinegar; salt and black pepper

Baked Peppers with Chorizo

■ Preheat the slow cooker if necessary, see manufacturer's instructions. Arrange the peppers, cut side uppermost in a single layer in the base of the slow cooker pot. Divide the spring onions and chorizo between the peppers, then pack in the cherry tomatoes.

■ Sprinkle with the garlic and torn basil, then add a pinch of paprika to each one, a drizzle of balsamic vinegar and a little salt and pepper.

■ Cover with the lid and cook on High for 3-4 hours until the peppers are softened. Lift out of the slow cooker pot with a fish slice, arrange on a platter, serve hot or cold sprinkled with extra basil leaves.

MAKE A VEGGIE VERSION

For baked pepper pizzas, omit the chorizo and smoked hot paprika, bake as for the main recipe, then transfer the peppers to a shallow ovenproof dish, tear a drained 150 g (5 oz) pack of mozzarella into small pieces, sprinkle over the pepper, then brown under a hot grill for 4–5 minutes. Garnish with torn basil leaves and stoned black olives.

SERVES 4

Preparation time 25 minutes
Cooking temperature Low
Cooking time 6–8 hours

INGREDIENTS

1	**500 g (1 lb) turkey breast, diced**
2	**juice of 1 large orange**
3	**½ teaspoon ground mixed spice**
4	**2 tablespoons, 25 g (1 oz), dried cranberries**
5	**500 g (1 lb) prepared weight pumpkin, cut into 2.5 cm (1 inch) cubes**

STORECUPBOARD

1 tablespoon sunflower oil; 1 onion, chopped; 2 teaspoons plain flour; 300 ml (½ pint) chicken stock; salt and black pepper

Thanksgiving Turkey with Pumpkin

■ Preheat the slow cooker if necessary, see manufacturer's instructions. Heat the oil in a large frying pan, then add the turkey a few pieces at a time. Add the onion and fry for 5 minutes, stirring until golden.

■ Sprinkle the flour over, then stir in. Pour in the stock and orange juice, then mix in the mixed spice, dried cranberries and salt and pepper. Bring to the boil, stirring.

■ Add the pumpkin to the slow cooker pot, pour over the turkey mix and press the turkey beneath the surface of the stock. Cover and cook on Low for 6–8 hours until the turkey is fully cooked. Spoon into shallow dishes and serve with steamed green beans and broccoli, if liked.

SERVES 4

Preparation time 15 minutes
Cooking temperature High and Low
Cooking time 7–8 hours

INGREDIENTS

1   4 pork chops, about 750 g (1½ lb) in total

2   2 dessert apples, peeled, cored and quartered

3   3 teaspoons English mustard

4   6 medium potatoes (for mashed potato)

5   handful chopped chives (optional)

STORECUPBOARD

3 tablespoons apple balsamic or plain balsamic vinegar; 2 tablespoons light muscovado sugar; 2 onions, thinly sliced; 2 tablespoons cornflour; 200 ml (7 fl oz) boiling chicken stock

Balsamic Braised Pork Chops

■ Preheat the slow cooker if necessary, see manufacturer's instructions. Put the pork chops into the base of the slow cooker pot and spoon over the vinegar and sugar. Sprinkle the onions on top, then add the apples.

■ Mix the cornflour and mustard with a little cold water to make a smooth paste, then gradually stir in the boiling stock until smooth. Pour over the pork. Cover with the lid and cook on High for 30 minutes. Reduce the heat and cook on Low for 6½– 7½ hours, or set to auto for 7–8 hours, until the pork is cooked through and tender.

■ Peel the potatoes and cut into small evenly-sized pieces. Boil in salted water until soft, about 25 minutes, and mash until smooth.

■ Transfer the pork and mashed potato to serving plates, stir the sauce and spoon over the chops. Sprinkle with chopped chives, if liked.

REPLACE VINEGAR WITH CIDER

For cider braised pork, prepare pork chops as for the main recipe, omitting the vinegar. Bring 200 ml (7 fl oz) dry cider to the boil. Make up the cornflour paste, then gradually stir in the boiling cider instead of the stock. Pour over the chops and continue as for the main recipe.

Preparation time 20 minutes
Cooking temperature High
Cooking time 5–6 hours

INGREDIENTS

1	1.25 kg (2½ lb) lean pork ribs

2	1 large carrot, sliced

3	3 bay leaves

4	100 g (3½ oz) ready-made jerk glaze

STORECUPBOARD

1 onion, cut into wedges; 2 tablespoons malt vinegar; salt and black pepper; 2 spring onions, sliced

Sticky Jerk Ribs

■ Preheat the slow cooker if necessary, see manufacturer's instructions. Add the pork ribs, onion and carrot to the slow cooker pot, then add the bay leaves and vinegar. Season the mixture with plenty of salt and pepper, then pour over enough boiling water to cover the ribs, making sure that the level is about 2.5 cm (1 inch) from the top of the pot.

■ Cover with the lid and cook on High for 5–6 hours, or until the meat is beginning to fall away from the bones.

■ Lift the ribs out of the slow cooker pot with tongs and put into a foil lined grill pan or baking sheet.

■ Brush the glaze over the ribs and scatter the spring onions over. Cook under a preheated grill with the ribs about 5 cm (2 inches) away from the heat for about 10 minutes, turning and brushing with the pan juices and a little oil until a deep brown. Transfer to plates and serve.

SERVES 4

Preparation time 15 minutes
Cooking temperature Low
Cooking time 8¼–10¼ hours

INGREDIENTS

1	**4 chicken thigh and 4 chicken drumstick joints**
2	**4 rashers smoked back bacon, diced**
3	**400 g (13 oz) leeks, thinly sliced; white and green parts kept separate**
4	**3 teaspoons wholegrain mustard**
5	**mashed potato, to serve**

STORECUPBOARD

2 tablespoons sunflower oil; 2 tablespoons plain flour; 600 ml (1 pint) chicken stock; salt and black pepper

Mustard Chicken & Bacon

■ Preheat the slow cooker if necessary, see manufacturer's instructions. Heat the oil in a frying pan, add the chicken joints and fry over a high heat until browned. Transfer to the slow cooker pot with a slotted spoon.

■ Add the bacon and white sliced leeks to the frying pan and fry, stirring, for 5 minutes or until just beginning to turn golden. Stir in the flour, then gradually mix in the stock, mustard and a little salt and pepper. Bring to the boil. Pour into the slow cooker pot, cover with the lid and cook on Low for 8–10 hours.

■ Add the green leeks and stir into the sauce, then replace the lid and cook, still on Low, for 15 minutes or until the green leeks are just softened. Serve in shallow serving bowls with mashed potato.

MAKE IT WITH FRANKFURTERS

For mustard chicken & frankfurter casserole, fry the chicken, then drain and add to the slow cooker pot. Add 1 chopped onion and 4 chilled sliced frankfurters to the pan and fry for 5 minutes. Stir in the flour, then gradually mix in the stock, mustard and seasoning. Add a 200 g (7 oz) can of drained sweetcorn in place of leek, transfer to the slow cooker pot and cook on Low for 8–10 hours.

PUDDINGS

SERVES 4-5

Preparation time 30 minutes, plus chilling
Cooking temperature High
Cooking time 2–2½ hours

INGREDIENTS

1	**8 trifle sponges**
2	**300 g (10 oz) full-fat cream cheese**
3	**150 ml (¼ pint) double cream**
4	**3 eggs**
5	**300 g (10 oz) fresh strawberries, sliced**

STORECUPBOARD

75 g (3 oz) caster sugar; grated rind and juice of
½ lemon plus 1 tablespoon lemon juice

Strawberry Cheesecake

■ Preheat the slow cooker if necessary, see manufacturer's instructions. Line the base and sides of a soufflé dish, 14 cm (5½ inches) in diameter and 9 cm (3½ inches) high, with nonstick baking paper, checking first it will fit in the slow cooker pot. Line the base with the trifle sponges, trimming them to fit in a single layer.

■ Put the cream cheese and sugar in a bowl, then gradually whisk in the cream until smooth and thick. Gradually whisk in the eggs one at a time, then mix in the ½ lemon rind and juice. Pour the mixture into the dish and spread it level.

■ Cover the top with buttered foil and lower it into the slow cooker pot. Pour boiling water into the pot to come halfway up the sides of the dish. Cover with the lid and cook on High for 2–2½ hours or until the cheesecake is well risen and softly set in the centre.

■ Lift the dish out of the slow cooker pot using a tea towel and leave to cool and firm up. The cheesecake will sink quickly as it cools to about the size that it was before cooking. Transfer to the refrigerator to chill for at least 4 hours.

■ When ready to serve, loosen the edge of the cheesecake with a knife, turn out on to a serving plate, peel off the lining paper and turn it the right way up. Mix the tablespoon of lemon juice and the sliced strawberries in a bowl and toss together. Spoon on top of the cheesecake and serve immediately.

SERVES 4

Preparation time 20 minutes, plus chilling
Cooking temperature Low
Cooking time 2½–3½ hours

INGREDIENTS

1	butter, for greasing

2	2 eggs, plus 3 egg yolks

3	400 g (13 oz) can full-fat condensed milk

4	125 ml (4 fl oz) semi-skimmed milk

STORECUPBOARD

125 g (4 oz) granulated sugar; 125 ml (4 fl oz) water; 2 tablespoons boiling water; grated rind of ½ small lemon

Crème Caramels

■ Preheat the slow cooker if necessary, see manufacturer's instructions. Lightly butter 4 metal individual pudding moulds, each 250 ml (8 fl oz). Pour the sugar and cold water into a small saucepan and heat gently, stirring occasionally until the sugar has completely dissolved.

■ Increase the heat and boil the syrup for 5 minutes, without stirring, until golden (keep a watchful eye as it cooks). Take off the heat, add the boiling water and stand well back. Tilt the pan to mix, and when bubbles have subsided pour into the pudding moulds to coat the base and sides.

■ Put the eggs and egg yolks into a bowl and fork together. Pour the condensed milk and fresh milk into a saucepan, bring to the boil, then gradually beat into the egg

mixture until smooth. Strain back into the pan, then stir in the lemon rind.

■ Pour the custard into the syrup-lined pudding moulds, then transfer the moulds into the slow cooker pot. Cover the top of each one with a square of foil. Pour hot water around the moulds so that the water comes halfway up the sides, then cover with the lid and cook on Low for 2½–3½ hours or until the custard is set with just a slight wobble in the centre. Lift out of the slow cooker pot with a tea towel, cool, then transfer to the refrigerator for 3–4 hours or overnight to chill.

■ To serve, dip the base of the moulds into boiling water for 10 seconds, loosen the top of the custard with a fingertip, then turn out on to rimmed plates.

Preparation time 20 minutes
Cooking temperature High
Cooking time 1¼–1½ hours

INGREDIENTS

1	**125 g (4 oz) plain dark chocolate, plus 8 extra small squares**
2	**75 g (3 oz) butter**
3	**2 eggs plus 2 egg yolks**
4	**½ teaspoon vanilla extract**
5	**vanilla ice cream or crème fraîche**

STORECUPBOARD

75 g (3 oz) caster sugar; 40 g (1½ oz) plain flour;
sifted icing sugar

Chocolate Brownie Puddings

■ Preheat the slow cooker if necessary, see manufacturer's instructions. Break the 125 g (4 oz) chocolate into pieces, put into a saucepan with the butter and heat gently, stirring occasionally, until melted. Take off the heat and set aside.

■ Whisk together the whole eggs, egg yolks, sugar and vanilla extract in a large bowl with an electric whisk for 3–4 minutes or until light and frothy. Gradually whisk in the melted chocolate mixture.

■ Sift the flour into the chocolate mix and fold together. Pour into 4 buttered and base-lined individual metal pudding moulds, each 250 ml (8 fl oz). Press 2 squares of chocolate into the centre of each, then loosely cover the tops with squares of buttered foil.

■ Transfer the pudding moulds to the slow cooker pot and pour boiling water into the pot to come halfway up the sides of the moulds. Cover with the lid and cook on High for 1¼–1½ hours until well risen and the tops spring back when lightly pressed.

■ Loosen the puddings with a knife, turn out into shallow serving dishes and remove the lining paper. Sprinkle with sifted icing sugar. Serve with spoonfuls of vanilla ice cream or crème fraîche.

MAKE IT FRUITY

For brandied cherry brownie puddings, soak 8 drained canned pitted black cherries in 1 tablespoon of brandy for at least 2 hours. Make the mixture as for the main recipe, dropping 2 cherries into the centre of each instead of the chocolate.

SERVES 4–5

Preparation time 30 minutes
Cooking temperature High
Cooking time 3–3½ hours

INGREDIENTS

1	**75 g (3 oz) butter, diced**
2	**2 eggs**
3	**2 tablespoons milk**
4	**1 dessert apple, cored and finely chopped**
5	**vanilla ice cream, crème fraîche or pouring cream, to serve**

STORECUPBOARD

150 g (5 oz) self-raising flour; 225 g (7½ oz) dark muscovado sugar; 300 ml (½ pint) boiling water

Sticky Toffee Apple Pudding

■ Preheat the slow cooker if necessary, see manufacturer's instructions. Butter the inside of a soufflé dish that is 14 cm (5½ inches) across and 9 cm (3½ inches) high, checking first that it will fit into the slow cooker pot. Put the flour in a bowl, add the 50 g(2 oz) butter and rub in with the fingertips until the mixture resembles fine breadcrumbs. Stir in 100 g (3½ oz) sugar, then mix in the eggs and milk until smooth. Stir in the apple.

■ Spoon the mixture into the soufflé dish and spread the tops to level. Sprinkle the remaining sugar over the top and dot with the remaining butter. Pour the measured boiling water over the top, then cover loosely with foil.

■ Lower the dish carefully into the slow cooker pot using a string handle or foil straps. Pour boiling water into the pot so that it comes halfway up the sides of the soufflé dish. Cover and cook on High for 3–3½ hours or until the sponge is well risen and the sauce is bubbling around the edges.

■ Lift the dish out of the slow cooker. Remove the foil and loosen the sides of the sponge. Cover with a dish that is large enough to catch the sauce, then invert and remove the soufflé dish. Serve with spoonfuls of vanilla ice cream, crème fraîche or pouring cream.

TRY BANANAS

For sticky banana pudding, prepare the pudding as for the main recipe but replace the chopped apple with 1 small, ripe and roughly mashed banana. Make up the sauce and cook as for the main recipe.

SERVES 6

Preparation time 20 minutes, plus cooling
Cooking temperature Low
Cooking time 3–4 hours

INGREDIENTS

1 250 g (8 oz) ready-to-eat dried apricots

2 grated rind and juice of 1 orange

3 2 x 135 g (4½ oz) pots ready-made custard

4 500 g (1 lb) natural yogurt

STORECUPBOARD

2 tablespoons caster sugar; 300 ml (½ pint) cold water

Apricot & Orange Fool

■ Preheat the slow cooker if necessary, see manufacturer's instructions. Put the apricots, orange rind and juice and sugar into the slow cooker pot and pour over the water. Cover with the lid and cook on Low for 3–4 hours until the apricots are plump.

■ Lift the pot out of the housing using oven gloves and leave the apricots to cool, then purée with a stick blender or transfer to a liquidizer and whizz until smooth.

■ Fold the custard and yogurt together until just mixed, then add the apricot purée and very lightly mix for a marbled effect. Spoon into the glasses and serve with dainty biscuits if liked.

ADJUST THE FOOL FLAVOURS

For prune & vanilla fool, put 250 g
(8 oz) ready-to-eat stoned prunes,
1 teaspoon vanilla extract, 2
tablespoons honey and 300 ml
(½ pint) cold water in the slow
cooker pot and cook, cool and make
up the fool as for the main recipe.

SERVES 6

Preparation time 15 minutes, plus chilling
Cooking temperature Low
Cooking time 2–2½ hours

INGREDIENTS

1   **2 eggs, plus 3 egg yolks**

2   **300 ml (½ pint) double cream**

3   **150 g (5 oz) blueberries, to serve**

STORECUPBOARD

100 g (3½ oz) caster sugar; grated rind of
2 lemons and the juice of 1 lemon

Lemon Custard Creams

■ Preheat the slow cooker if necessary, see manufacturer's instructions. Put the eggs and egg yolks, sugar and lemon rind into a bowl and whisk together until just mixed.

■ Pour the cream into a small saucepan, bring just to the boil, then gradually whisk into the egg mixture. Strain the lemon juice and gradually whisk into the cream mixture.

■ Pour the mixture into 6 small tea cups and put them in the slow cooker pot. Pour hot water into the pot so that it comes halfway up the sides of the cups. Loosely cover the tops of the cups with a piece of foil, cover the slow cooker with the lid and cook on Low for 2–2½ hours or until the custards are just set.

■ Lift the cups carefully out of the slow cooker with a tea towel and leave to cool.

Transfer to the refrigerator to chill for 3–4 hours or overnight.

■ Set the cups on their saucers and decorate the tops of the custard with blueberries.

TRY IT WITH ELDERFLOWER

For lime & elderflower custard creams, make the puddings as for the main recipe but with the grated rind and juice of 2 limes and 2 tablespoons undiluted elderflower cordial instead of the lemon rind and juice. Cook in coffee cups, then serve chilled with fresh strawberries drizzled with a little extra elderflower cordial.

SERVES 4

Preparation time 20 minutes
Cooking temperature Low
Cooking time 3–4 hours

INGREDIENTS

1 300 ml (½ pint) cloudy apple juice

2 large pinch of saffron threads

3 4 cardamom pods, roughly crushed

4 4 firm, ripe pears

5 8 tablespoons readymade chocolate sauce

STORECUPBOARD

3 tablespoons caster sugar

Saffron Pears with Chocolate

■ Preheat the slow cooker if necessary, see manufacturer's instructions. Pour the apple juice into a small saucepan, add the sugar, saffron and cardamom pods and their tiny black seeds. Bring to the boil, then tip into the slow cooker pot.

■ Peel the pears and cut each in half lengthways, leaving the stalk on. Remove the pear cores with a melon baller, if you have one, or a teaspoon. Add the pears to the slow cooker pot, pressing them beneath the surface of the liquid as much as you can. Cover with the lid and cook on Low for 3–4 hours or until the pears are tender and pale yellow.

■ When ready to serve, spoon the pears and some of the saffron sauce into shallow dishes, pour the chocolate sauce into a small jug and allow dinner guests to drizzle the sauce over the pears just before eating.

FOR A WARMING VERSION

For spiced pears with red wine, warm 150 ml (¼ pint) red wine with 50 g (2 oz) caster sugar, 150 ml (¼ pint) water, the pared rind of ½ small orange, 1 small cinnamon stick, halved, and 4 cloves. Pour into the slow cooker pot, add 4 halved, peeled and cored pears, cover and cook as for the main recipe.

Preparation time 25 minutes
Cooking temperature High
Cooking time 3½–4 hours

INGREDIENTS

| 1 | 150 g (5 oz) vegetable suet |

| 2 | 200–250 ml (7–8 fl oz) milk or milk and water mixed |

| 3 | 4 tablespoons strawberry jam |

| 4 | 1 x 425 g (15 oz) can of ready-made custard |

STORECUPBOARD

300 g (10 oz) self-raising flour; 50 g (2 oz) caster sugar; grated rind of 2 lemons; salt

Jam Roly-poly Pudding

■ Preheat the slow cooker if necessary, see manufacturer's instructions. Put the flour, suet, sugar, lemon rind and a pinch of salt in a bowl and mix well. Gradually stir in the milk or milk and water to make a soft but not sticky dough. Knead lightly, then roll out on a piece of floured nonstick baking paper to a rectangle about 23 x 30 cm (9 x 12 inches). Turn the paper so that the shorter edges are facing you.

■ Spread the jam over the pastry, leaving 2 cm (¾ inch) around the edges. Roll up, starting at a shorter edge, using the paper to help. Wrap in the paper, then in a sheet of foil. Twist the ends together tightly, leaving space for the pudding to rise.

■ Transfer the pudding to the slow cooker pot and raise off the base by standing it on 2 ramekin dishes. Pour boiling water into the pot to come a little up the sides of the pudding, being careful that the water cannot seep through any joins. Cover with the lid and cook on High for 3½–4 hours or until the pudding is light and fluffy. Lift out of the pot, then unwrap and cut into thick slices. Serve with hot custard.

ADD RAISINS

For spotted dick, grate the rind of 1 large orange and reserve, squeeze the juice into a saucepan, bring to the boil, add 150 g (5 oz) raisins and leave to soak for 30 minutes. Make up the pastry as for the main recipe, adding the orange rind, the grated rind of 1 lemon and the soaked raisins before mixing with milk to make a soft dough. Shape into 23 cm (9 inches) long log. Wrap in nonstick baking paper and foil, then cook as for the main recipe.

SERVES 4–6

Preparation time 15 minutes
Cooking temperature Low and High
Cooking time 1¼–1¾ hours

INGREDIENTS

1	150 ml (¼ pint) Marsala or sweet sherry

2	6 firm, ripe peaches or nectarines, halved and stones removed

3	1 vanilla pod, slit lengthways

4	125 g (4 oz) raspberries

STORECUPBOARD

150 ml (¼ pint) water; 75 g (3 oz) caster sugar;
2 teaspoons cornflour

Peaches with Marsala & Vanilla

■ Preheat the slow cooker if necessary, see manufacturer's instructions. Put the Marsala or sherry, the water and sugar in a saucepan and bring to the boil.

■ Put the peach or nectarine halves and vanilla pod in the slow cooker pot and pour in the hot syrup. Cover with the lid and cook on Low for 1–1½ hours or until hot and the fruit is tender.

■ Lift the fruit out of the slow cooker pot and transfer to a serving dish. Remove the vanilla pod, then scrape the black seeds from the pod with a small sharp knife and stir the seeds back into the cooking syrup. Mix the cornflour to a smooth paste with a little cold water, then stir into the cooking syrup and cook on High for 15 minutes, stirring occasionally.

■ Pour the thickened syrup over the fruit, sprinkle with the raspberries and serve warm or chilled.

TRY APPLES AND PEARS

For poached apples & pears with Marsala & vanilla, make the Marsala syrup as for the main recipe. Peel, core and quarter 3 Braeburn dessert apples and 3 just-ripe pears. Add the fruit to the slow cooker pot with a slit vanilla pod and pour over the hot syrup. Cook and thicken the syrup as for the main recipe.

SERVES 4

Preparation time 20 minutes
Cooking temperature High
Cooking time 1–1¼ hours

INGREDIENTS

1 4 nectarines, halved, stoned and flesh diced

2 250 g (8 oz) strawberries, halved or quartered depending on size

3 finely grated rind and juice of 2 oranges

4 150 g (5 oz) mascarpone cheese

5 40 g (1½ oz) amaretti biscuits

STORECUPBOARD

50 g (2 oz) caster sugar, plus 2 tablespoons; 125 ml (4 fl oz) cold water

Compote with Mascarpone

■ Preheat the slow cooker if necessary, see manufacturer's instructions. Put the nectarines and strawberries in the slow cooker pot with 50 g (2 oz) sugar, the rind of 1 orange, the juice of 1½ oranges and the measured water. Cover and cook on High for 1–1¼ hours or until the fruit is tender. Serve warm or cold.

■ Just before the compote is ready, mix the mascarpone with the remaining sugar, orange rind and juice. Reserve some of the amaretti biscuits for decoration. Crumble the rest with your fingertips into the bowl with the mascarpone and stir until mixed. Spoon the fruit into tumblers, top with spoonfuls of the orange mascarpone mixture and decorate with a sprinkling of amaretti biscuit crumbs.

CHANGE THE FRUIT FLAVOURS

For plum & cranberry compote with orange mascarpone, replace the nectarines and strawberries with 625g (1¼ lb) plums, quartered and stoned, and 125 g (4 oz) cranberries (no need to thaw if frozen). Increase the sugar to 75 g (3 oz), then follow the main recipe, using cranberry and raspberry juice instead of water, if liked.

Preparation time 25 minutes
Cooking temperature High
Cooking time 4½–5 hours

INGREDIENTS

1   **125 g (4 oz) butter, at room temperature, plus extra for greasing**

2   **2 eggs, beaten**

3   **2 tablespoons poppy seeds**

4   **170 g (6 oz) crème fraîche, to serve**

STORECUPBOARD

250 g (8 oz) caster sugar; 125 g (4 oz) self-raising flour; grated rind of 1 lemon, plus juice of 1½ lemons and lemon rind curls, to decorate

Lemon & Poppy Seed Drizzle Cake

■ Preheat the slow cooker if necessary, see manufacturer's instructions. Lightly butter a soufflé dish that is 14 cm (5½ inches) across the base and 9 cm (3½ inches) high, and base-line with a circle of nonstick baking paper, making sure it will fit into the slow cooker pot.

■ Cream together 125 g (4 oz) each butter and sugar in a bowl with a wooden spoon or electric hand mixer. Gradually mix in alternate spoonfuls of beaten egg and flour, and continue adding and beating until the mixture is smooth. Stir in the poppy seeds and lemon rind, then spoon the mixture into the soufflé dish and spread to level. Cover the top of the dish loosely with buttered foil and then lower into the slow cooker pot.

■ Pour boiling water into the slow cooker pot so that it comes halfway up the sides of the dish. Cover with the lid and cook on High for 4½–5 hours or until the cake is dry and springs back when pressed gently with a fingertip.

■ Lift the dish carefully out of the slow cooker, remove the foil and loosen the edge of the cake with a knife. Turn out on to a plate or shallow dish with a rim. Quickly warm the lemon juice and the remaining sugar together for the syrup and as soon as the sugar has dissolved, pour the syrup over the cake. Leave to cool and for the syrup to soak in. Cut into slices and serve with spoonfuls of crème fraîche, decorated with lemon rind curls.

ADD MORE CITRUS FLAVOURS

For citrus drizzle cake, omit the lemon rind and poppy seeds from the cake mixture and stir in the grated rind of ½ lemon, ½ lime and ½ small orange. Bake as for the main recipe. Make the syrup using the juice of the grated fruits and sugar.

SERVES 4

Preparation time 25 minutes
Cooking temperature High
Cooking time 1–1¼ hours

INGREDIENTS

1 200 g (7 oz) plain dark chocolate, broken into pieces

2 50 g (2 oz) butter, plus extra for greasing

3 4 eggs, separated

4 6 tablespoons double cream

5 4 teaspoons chopped mint

STORECUPBOARD

4 tablespoons caster sugar; 1 tablespoons warm water; sifted icing sugar, to decorate

Hot Chocolate Mousses

■ Preheat the slow cooker if necessary, see manufacturer's instructions. Put the chocolate and butter in a bowl, set over a saucepan of very gently simmering water making sure that the water does not touch the base of the bowl and leave until just melted.

■ Meanwhile, butter 4 cups, each 250 ml (8 fl oz), checking first that they will fit in the slow cooker pot.

■ Whisk the egg whites in a bowl until soft peaks form, then gradually whisk in the sugar a teaspoonful at a time until it has all been added and the meringue is thick and glossy. Take the bowl of chocolate off the saucepan, stir in the egg yolks and warm water and gently fold in a spoonful of the egg whites to loosen the mixture. Fold in the remaining egg whites, then divide between the cups.

■ Cover the tops with domed foil and put into the slow cooker pot. Pour boiling water into the pot to come halfway up the sides of the cups. Cover with the lid and cook on High for 1–1¼ hours or until the puddings are softly set in the centre.

■ Lift the puddings out of the slow cooker pot and remove the foil. Mix the cream and mint together and pour into a jug. Dust the puddings with icing sugar and serve immediately with the mint cream.

TRY IT WITH GINGER

For gingered mousses, add 4 teaspoons finely chopped stem ginger to the mousse mixture and cook as for the main recipe. To serve, stir an extra 2 teaspoons finely chopped stem ginger into 6 tablespoons crème fraîche in a bowl.

SERVES 4

Preparation time 30 minutes, plus chilling
Cooking temperature Low
Cooking time 2½–3½ hours

INGREDIENTS

1   **4 egg yolks**

2   **400 ml (14 fl oz) double cream**

3   **¼ teaspoon peppermint extract**

4   **150 g (5 oz) raspberries**

STORECUPBOARD

40 g (1½ oz) caster sugar; 2 tablespoons icing sugar

Peppermint & Raspberry Brûlée

■ Preheat the slow cooker if necessary, see manufacturer's instructions. Whisk the egg yolks and sugar in a bowl for 3–4 minutes until frothy, then gradually whisk in the cream. Stir in the peppermint extract, then strain the egg custard into a jug.

■ Pour into 4 ramekin dishes, each 150 ml (¼ pint), checking first that they will fit in the slow cooker pot. Put the dishes into the pot and pour in boiling water to come halfway up the sides of the dishes, then loosely cover the top of each dish with foil.

■ Cover with the lid and cook on Low for 2½–3½ hours or until the custard is set with a slight quiver to the middle. Lift the dishes carefully out of the slow cooker and leave to cool. Transfer to the refrigerator to chill for 4 hours.

■ When ready to serve, pile a few raspberries in the centre of each dish and sprinkle over some icing sugar. Caramelize the sugar with a cook's blow torch.

MAKE IT CHOCOLATEY

For peppermint & white chocolate brûlée, bring 350 ml (12 fl oz) double cream just to the boil in a saucepan, take off the heat and add 100 g (4 oz) good-quality white chocolate, broken into pieces, and leave until melted. Whisk the egg yolks with 25 g (1 oz) caster sugar, then gradually mix in the chocolate cream and the peppermint extract. Continue as for the main recipe. Replace the raspberries with blueberries and serve as for the main recipe.

Preparation time 10 minutes
Cooking temperature Low
Cooking time 2½–3 hours

INGREDIENTS

1   **750 ml (1¼ pints) full-fat milk**

2   **3 tablespoons set honey**

3   **125 g (4 oz) risotto rice**

4   **4 tablespoons of apricot conserve**

5   **4 tablespoons of double cream**

STORECUPBOARD

1 tablespoon sunflower oil, for greasing

Honeyed Rice Pudding

■ Preheat the slow cooker if necessary, see manufacturer's instructions. Lightly grease the inside of the slow cooker pot with the oil. Pour the milk into a saucepan, add the honey and bring just to the boil, stirring until the honey has melted. Pour into the slow cooker pot, add the rice and stir gently.

■ Cover with the lid and cook on Low for 2½–3 hours, stirring once during cooking, or until the pudding is thickened and the rice is soft. Stir again just before spooning into dishes and serve topped with spoonfuls of apricot conserve and whipped double cream.

FOR A VANILLA PUDDING

For vanilla rice pudding, pour the milk into a saucepan, replace the honey with 3 tablespoons caster sugar and bring just to the boil. Slit a vanilla pod, scrape the black seeds out with a small knife and add to the milk with the pod. Pour into the greased slow cooker pot, add the rice and cook as for the main recipe. Remove the vanilla pod before serving with thick cream.

Preparation time 10 minutes
Cooking temperature Low
Cooking time 1½–2 hours

INGREDIENTS

1	25 g (1 oz) butter
2	grated rind and juice of 1 lime plus curls of lime rind, to decorate
3	1 vanilla pod or 1 teaspoon vanilla extract
4	3 tablespoons white or dark rum
5	6 small bananas, peeled and halved lengthways

STORECUPBOARD

75 g (3 oz) light muscovado sugar; 200 ml
(7 fl oz) boiling water

Sticky Rum Bananas with Vanilla

■ Preheat the slow cooker if necessary, see manufacturer's instructions. Add the butter, sugar and lime rind and juice to the warming slow cooker pot and stir until the butter has melted.

■ Slit the vanilla pod along its length, open it out flat with a small sharp knife and scrape the tiny black seeds away from inside the pod. Add the seeds and the pod or vanilla extract, if using, to the slow cooker pot along with the rum and the boiling water.

■ Add the bananas to the slow cooker pot, arranging them in a single layer and pressing them beneath the liquid as much as you can. Cover with the lid and cook on Low for 1½–2 hours or until the bananas are hot.

■ Spoon the bananas and rum sauce into dishes and decorate with extra lime rind curls.

MAKE IT WITH PINEAPPLE

For sticky brandied pineapple, make up the vanilla syrup as for the main recipe, replacing the rum with brandy. Trim the top off a medium pineapple, cut away the skin and eyes, and slice, then halve each slice, cutting away the core. Press it beneath the syrup. Cover and cook as for the main recipe.

SERVES 4-6

Preparation time 15 minutes
Cooking temperature High
Cooking time 3-3½ hours

INGREDIENTS

1 butter, for greasing

2 40 g (1 oz) desiccated coconut

3 400 g (13 oz) can cherry pie filling

4 500 g (1 lb) pack Madeira cake mix

5 1 egg

STORECUPBOARD

4 tablespoons sunflower oil

Cherry & Coconut Sponge Pudding

■ Preheat the slow cooker if necessary, see manufacturer's instructions. Lightly butter a 1.5 litre (2½ pint) pudding basin and base-line with a circle of nonstick baking paper, checking first it will fit in the slow cooker pot. Sprinkle in a little of the coconut, then tilt and turn the basin until the buttery sides are lightly coated. Spoon half the cherry pie filling into the base of the basin.

■ Tip the Madeira cake mix into a bowl and mix together with the oil or egg and water according to the pack instructions. Stir in the remaining coconut, then spoon the mixture into the basin and spread it level. Cover the top with buttered, domed foil and lower the basin into the slow cooker pot.

■ Pour boiling water into the slow cooker pot to come halfway up the sides of the basin. Cover with the lid and cook on High for 3-3½ hours or until the sponge is well risen, feels dry and springs back when pressed with a fingertip.

■ Lift the basin out of the slow cooker pot using a tea towel and remove the foil. Loosen the edge of the pudding with a knife, turn out on to a plate and peel off the lining paper. Heat the remaining pie filling in a small saucepan or the microwave until hot. Serve the pudding in bowls with the warm cherries.

USE A CHOCOLATE CAKE MIX

For spiced chocolate cherry sponge pudding, line the pudding basin with cherry pie filling as for the main recipe, omitting the coconut. Make up a 500 g (1 lb) chocolate-flavoured Madeira cake mix with 1 teaspoon ground cinnamon and the sunflower oil or egg and continue as for the main recipe.

SERVES 4

Preparation time 15 minutes
Cooking temperature Low
Cooking time 2–3 hours

INGREDIENTS

1	**8 clementines**
2	**50 g (2 oz) honey**
3	**4 tablespoons whisky**
4	**15 g (½ oz) butter**

STORECUPBOARD

75 g (3 oz) light muscovado sugar; grated rind and juice of ½ lemon; 300 ml (½ pint) boiling water

Hot Toddy Oranges

■ Preheat the slow cooker if necessary, see manufacturer's instructions. Peel the clementines, leaving them whole. Put the remaining ingredients in the slow cooker pot and mix together.

■ Add the clementines. Cover the pot with the lid and cook on Low for 2–3 hours or until piping hot. Spoon into shallow bowls and serve.

FOR AN APRICOT VERSION

For hot toddy apricots, put all the ingredients, omitting the clementines and sugar, into the slow cooker pot as for the main recipe. Add 300 g (10 oz) ready-to-eat dried apricots and continue as for the main recipe.

Preparation time 10 minutes
Cooking temperature High
Cooking time 1–1½ hours

INGREDIENTS

| **1** | **50 g (2 oz) butter** |

| **2** | **2 tablespoons golden syrup** |

| **3** | **4 dessert apples, cored and each cut into 8 slices** |

| **4** | **375 g (12 oz) pack or 6 ready-made pancakes** |

| **5** | **400 g (14 oz) vanilla ice cream, to serve** |

STORECUPBOARD

75 g (3 oz) light muscovado sugar; juice of 1 lemon

Toffee Apple Pancakes

■ Preheat the slow cooker if necessary, see manufacturer's instructions. Heat the butter, sugar and syrup in a saucepan or in a bowl in the microwave until the butter has just melted.

■ Add the apples and lemon juice to the slow cooker pot and toss together. Stir the butter mix and pour it over the apples. Cover with the lid and cook on High for 1–1½ hours or until the apples are tender but still holding their shape.

■ Heat the pancakes in a frying pan or the microwave, according to the pack instructions. Arrange on serving plates, folding the pancakes over. Stir the apple mix, then spoon it on to the pancakes. Top with a scoop of vanilla ice cream.

SWAP APPLES FOR BANANAS

For toffee banana pancakes, make as for the main recipe, replacing the apples with 6 small thickly sliced bananas and adding 150 ml (¼ pint) boiling water. When ready to serve, reheat 6 pancakes, spread with 3 tablespoons chocolate and hazelnut spread, then top with the bananas, omitting the ice cream.

DRINKS & PRESERVES

SERVES 6

Preparation time 10 minutes
Cooking temperature High and Low
Cooking time 3-4 hours

INGREDIENTS

1 1 litre (1¾ pints) cranberry and raspberry drink

2 250 g (8 oz) frozen berry fruits

3 4 tablespoons crème de cassis (optional)

4 4 small star anise

5 1 cinnamon stick, halved lengthways

STORECUPBOARD

50 g (2 oz) caster sugar

Hot Spiced Berry Punch

■ Preheat the slow cooker if necessary, see manufacturer's instructions. Pour the cranberry and raspberry drink into the slow cooker pot. Add the frozen fruits, the sugar and crème de cassis, if using. Stir together, then add the star anise and halved cinnamon stick.

■ Cover with the lid and cook on High for 1 hour. Reduce the heat and cook on Low for 2-3 hours, or set to auto for 3-4 hours, until piping hot.

■ Strain, if liked, then put the star anise and cinnamon into small heatproof glasses. Ladle the hot punch into the glasses.

Preparation time 10 minutes
Cooking temperature High and Low
Cooking time 3–4 hours

INGREDIENTS

1 1 litre (1¾ pints) dry cider

2 125 ml (4 fl oz) whisky

3 oranges freshly squeezed to make 125 ml (4 fl oz) orange juice, plus orange wedges and rind curls, to decorate

4 4 tablespoons set honey

5 2 cinnamon sticks

Cider Toddy

■ Preheat the slow cooker if necessary, see manufacturer's instructions. Add all the ingredients, except the orange wedges and rind curls, to the slow cooker pot, cover with the lid and cook on High for 1 hour.

■ Reduce the heat and cook on Low for 2–3 hours, or set to auto for 3–4 hours, until piping hot. Stir, discard the cinnamon sticks, then ladle into heatproof tumblers. Add orange wedges and curls to decorate, if liked.

TRY IT WITH GINGER

For citrus toddy, replace the whisky with 125 ml (4 fl oz) ginger wine and make as for the main recipe.

Preparation time 10 minutes
Cooking temperature Low
Cooking time 2–3 hours

INGREDIENTS

| 1 | 100 g (3½ oz) good-quality chocolate |

| 2 | 750 ml (1¼ pints) full-fat milk |

| 3 | few drops of vanilla extract |

| 4 | little ground cinnamon |

| 5 | mini marshmallows, to serve |

STORECUPBOARD

25 g (1 oz) caster sugar

Skier's Hot Chocolate

■ Preheat the slow cooker if necessary, see manufacturer's instructions. Put the chocolate and sugar in the slow cooker pot, add the milk, vanilla extract and cinnamon.

■ Cover with the lid and cook on Low for 2–3 hours, whisking once or twice, until the chocolate has melted and the drink is hot. Ladle into mugs and top with a few mini marshmallows.

Preparation time 10 minutes
Cooking temperature High and Low
Cooking time 3–4 hours

INGREDIENTS

1 25 g (1 oz) tartaric acid

2 fresh mint sprigs, to serve

STORECUPBOARD

3 lemons, washed and thinly sliced; 625 g (1¼ lb)
granulated sugar; 900 ml (1½ pints) boiling water

Lemon Cordial

■ Preheat the slow cooker if necessary, see manufacturer's instructions. Add the lemon slices to the slow cooker pot with the sugar and boiling water and stir well until the sugar is almost completely dissolved. Cover the pot with the lid and cook on High for 1 hour.

■ Reduce the heat and cook on Low for 2–3 hours or until the lemons are almost translucent. Switch off the slow cooker and stir in the tartaric acid. Leave to cool.

■ Remove and discard some of the sliced lemons using a slotted spoon. Transfer the cordial and remaining lemon slices to 2 sterilized screw-topped, wide-necked bottles or storage jars. Seal the bottles well, label and store in the refrigerator for up to 1 month.

■ To serve, dilute the cordial with water in a ratio of 1:3, adding a few of the sliced lemons for decoration, ice cubes and sprigs of fresh mint.

ADD LIME TO THE MIX

For lemon & lime cordial, prepare the cordial using 2 lemons and 2 limes, washed and thinly sliced (instead of 3 lemons). Serve diluted with sparkling mineral water and sprigs of mint.

Preparation time 10 minutes
Cooking temperature High and Low
Cooking time 3–4 hours

INGREDIENTS

1	juice of 3 limes, plus 1 lime, thinly sliced
2	300 ml (½ pint) dark rum
3	300 ml (½ pint) ginger wine
4	2 slices of pineapple, cored but skin left on and cut into pieces

STORECUPBOARD

600 ml (1 pint) cold water; 75 g (3 oz) caster sugar

Hot Jamaican Punch

■ Preheat the slow cooker if necessary, see manufacturer's instructions. Strain the lime juice into the slow cooker pot and discard the pips. Add the rum, ginger wine, water and sugar, cover and cook on High for 1 hour.

■ Reduce the heat to Low and cook for 2–3 hours until the punch is piping hot or until you are ready to serve. Stir well, then ladle into heatproof glasses and add a slice of lime and 2 pieces of pineapple to each glass, as shown on the right of the picture.

MAKE A RUM TODDY

For rum toddy, put the grated rind of 1 lemon and 1 orange and the juice of 3 lemons and 3 oranges into the slow cooker. Add 125 g (4 oz) set honey and the sugar. Increase the water to 750 ml (1¼ pints) and reduce the rum to 150 ml (¼ pint). Cook and serve as for the main recipe, adding a cinnamon stick if liked.

SERVES 4

Preparation time 15 minutes
Cooking temperature Low
Cooking time 3–4 hours

INGREDIENTS

1   4 cardamom pods, crushed

2   7.5 cm (3 inch) piece cinnamon stick, halved

3   2.5 cm (1 inch) piece root ginger, peeled, thinly sliced

4   4 pears, stalks left on, peeled, halved lengthways, cored

5   pared rind and juice of 1 orange

STORECUPBOARD

300 ml (½ pint) hot water; 4 teaspoons sugar; pared rind and juice of 1 lemon

Spiced Pear Compote

■ Preheat the slow cooker if needed, see manufacturer's instructions. Pour the hot water into the slow cooker pot, then mix in the green cardamom pods and their black seeds, the cinnamon stick pieces, ginger slices and sugar.

■ Add the pears, then the lemon and orange juice, then gently turn the pears in the juice and water. Turn them over so that the cut sides are downwards and under the liquid in a single tight-fitting layer. Cut the pared lemon and orange rind into very thin strips and sprinkle on top.

■ Cover with the lid and cook on Low for 3–4 hours until the pears are tender. If they were very firm to begin with, they may take a little longer to cook. Serve warm.

ADD BERRIES

For apple & blackberry jelly, put 750 g (1½ lb) cooking apples, washed and diced, into the slow cooker pot with 250 g (8 oz) blackberries, 125 ml (4 fl oz) lemon juice and the boiling water. Continue as for the main recipe, omitting the herbs. Serve with scones.

MAKES 6 JARS

Preparation time 45 minutes, plus overnight cooling
Cooking temperature Low
Cooking time 8–10 hours

INGREDIENTS

1	**1 kg (2 lb) Seville oranges**

2	**granary toast, to serve**

STORECUPBOARD

1.2 litres (2 pints) boiling water; 2 kg (4 lb) preserving or granulated sugar

Orange Marmalade

■ Preheat the slow cooker if necessary, see manufacturer's instructions. Put the whole oranges into the slow cooker pot, cover with the boiling water and put an upturned saucer on top of the oranges to stop them from floating.

■ Cover with the lid and cook on Low for 8–10 hours or until the oranges are tender. Lift the pot out of the housing using oven gloves and leave to cool overnight. The next day, lift the oranges out of the slow cooker pot, draining well. Cut into quarters, scoop out and discard the pips, then thinly slice the oranges.

■ Put the sliced oranges and the liquid from the slow cooker pot into a preserving pan or large saucepan, add the sugar and heat gently, stirring occasionally until the

sugar has completely dissolved. Increase the heat, and boil for 20–30 minutes or until setting point is reached.

■ Warm 6 clean jars in a low oven for 5 minutes. Ladle the hot marmalade into the warm jars, cover the surface with waxed discs, add cellophane jam pot covers and secure with elastic bands or screw the jar lids in place. Label and store in a cool place until required. Serve with the granary toast.

ADD SOME GINGER HEAT

For dark ginger orange marmalade, cook the Seville oranges with 75 g (3 oz) peeled and finely chopped fresh root ginger in the slow cooker as for the main recipe. Make up the marmalade with the sliced oranges and ginger as for the main recipe but using 1.5 kg (3½ lb) preserving or granulated sugar and 500 g (1 lb) light muscovado sugar.

MAKES 3 SMALL JARS

Preparation time 15 minutes
Cooking temperature Low
Cooking time 3–4 hours

INGREDIENTS

1   **125 g (4 oz) unsalted butter, diced**

2   **4 eggs, beaten**

3   **grated rind and juice of 2 limes**

4   **3 passion fruit, halved**

STORECUPBOARD

400 g (13 oz) caster sugar; grated rind of 2 lemons
juice of 1 lemon

Passion Fruit & Lime Curd

■ Preheat the slow cooker if necessary, see manufacturer's instructions. Put the butter and sugar in a large basin, checking first that it will fit into the slow cooker pot, then heat in the microwave until the butter has just melted. Alternatively, heat the butter and sugar in a saucepan and then pour into the basin.

■ Stir the sugar mix, then gradually whisk in the eggs, and then the lime rind and juice. Cover the basin with foil and lower into the slow cooker pot. Pour boiling water into the pot to come halfway up the sides of the basin. Cover with the lid and cook on Low for 3–4 hours, stirring once during cooking, until thick.

■ Stir once more, then scoop the passion fruit seeds out of the halved fruit with a teaspoon and stir them into the preserve.

■ Warm 3 clean jars in a low oven for 5 minutes. Ladle the preserve into the warm jars, cover the surface with waxed discs, add cellophane jam pot covers and secure with elastic bands or screw the lids in place. Label and leave to cool. The preserve can be stored for up to 2 weeks in the refrigerator.

Preparation time 15 minutes
Cooking temperature High
Cooking time 3–5 hours

INGREDIENTS

1 300 g (10 oz) ready-to-eat dried apricots, diced

2 4 peaches, halved, stoned and diced

3 ready-made croissants, to serve

STORECUPBOARD

250 g (8 oz) caster sugar; 300 ml (½ pint) boiling water

Apricot Conserve

■ Preheat the slow cooker if necessary, see manufacturer's instructions. Put the apricots, peaches, sugar and boiling water into the slow cooker pot and stir together.

■ Cover with the lid and cook on High for 3–5 hours, stirring once during cooking and then again at the end, until the fruit is soft and the liquid thick and syrupy, with a texture like chutney.

■ Warm 3 clean jars in a low oven for 5 minutes. Ladle the conserve into the warmed jars. Cover the surface of the jarred conserve with waxed discs, add cellophane jam pot covers and secure with elastic bands or screw the jar lids in place. Label and leave to cool. The conserve can be stored for up to 2 months in the refrigerator. Serve with warm croissants.

ADD ORANGES

For apricot & orange conserve, put 400 g (13 oz) dried apricots, the grated rind and juice of 1 large orange, the sugar and the boiling water in the slow cooker pot, omitting the peaches. Continue as for the main recipe.

Preparation time 25 minutes
Cooking temperature Low
Cooking time 3–4 hours

INGREDIENTS

| 1 | 125 g (4 oz) unsalted butter |

| 2 | grated rind and juice of 1 orange |

| 3 | grated rind and juice of 1 lime |

| 4 | 4 eggs, beaten |

STORECUPBOARD

400 g (13 oz) caster sugar; grated rind and juice of 2 lemons

Tangy Citrus Curd

■ Preheat the slow cooker if necessary, see manufacturer's instructions. Put the butter and sugar in a saucepan, add the fruit rinds, then strain in the juice. Heat gently for 2–3 minutes, stirring occasionally, until the butter has melted and the sugar has dissolved.

■ Pour the mixture into a basin that will fit comfortably in your slow cooker pot. Leave to cool for 10 minutes, then gradually strain in the eggs and mix well. Cover the basin with foil. Fold a large piece of kitchen foil into 3, then place it at the bottom of the pot with the ends sticking up to use as a strap and place the basin on top. Pour hot water into the cooker pot to come halfway up the sides of the basin. Cover with the lid and cook on Low for 3–4 hours or until the mixture is very thick. Stir once or twice during cooking if possible.

■ Warm 2 clean jars. Spoon in the citrus curd, place a waxed disc on top and leave to cool. Seal each jar with a screw-top lid or a cellophane jam pot cover and an elastic band, label and store in the refrigerator. Use within 3–4 weeks.

A TRADITIONAL LEMON CURD

For lemon curd, prepare as for the main recipe, but omit the orange and lime and use 3 lemons, rather than 2. Cook and store as for the main recipe.

Preparation time 20 minutes
Cooking temperature High
Cooking time 2–2½ hours

INGREDIENTS

1   **7 sprigs of rosemary**

2   **7 sprigs of thyme**

3   **7 small bay leaves**

4   **1.5 kg (3 lb) firm red plums, washed and pricked**

STORECUPBOARD

750 ml (1¼ pints) white wine vinegar; 500 g (1 lb) caster sugar; 4 garlic cloves, unpeeled; 1 teaspoon salt; ½ teaspoon peppercorns

Pickled Plums

■ Preheat the slow cooker if necessary, see manufacturer's instructions. Pour the vinegar and sugar into the slow cooker pot, then add 4 sprigs each of the rosemary and thyme and 4 bay leaves, the garlic, salt and peppercorns. Cover with the lid and cook on High for 2–2½ hours, stirring once or twice.

■ Warm 3 clean jars. Pack the plums tightly into the jars. Tuck the remaining fresh herbs into the jars. Strain in the hot vinegar, making sure that the plums are completely covered. Seal tightly with rubber seals and jar lids.

■ Label the jars and leave to cool. Transfer to a cool, dark cupboard and store for 3–4 weeks before using. Once opened, store in the refrigerator.

MAKES 4 X 400 G (13 OZ) JARS

Preparation time 20 minutes
Cooking temperature High
Cooking time 4–5 hours

INGREDIENTS

1   **1 kg (2 lb) cooking apples, peeled, cored and chopped**

2   **250 g (8 oz) blackberries**

STORECUPBOARD

500 g (1 lb) granulated sugar; grated rind of 1 lemon; 2 tablespoons water or lemon juice

Blackberry & Apple Jam

■ Preheat the slow cooker if necessary, see manufacturer's instructions. Put all the ingredients in the slow cooker pot, in the order listed. Cover with the lid and cook on High for 4–5 hours, stirring once or twice during cooking. By the end of the cooking time the fruit should be thick and pulpy.

■ Warm 4 clean jars. Spoon in the jam, place a waxed disc on top and leave to cool. Seal each jar with a cellophane jam pot cover and an elastic band, label and store for up to 2 months in the refrigerator. (The jam's low sugar content means that it does not keep as long as conventional jam and must be kept in the refrigerator.)

ADD BERRIES

For apple, plum & mixed berry jam, replace half of the apples with 500 g (1 lb) stoned and chopped red plums and half the blackberries with 125 g (4 oz) raspberries. Cook and store as for the main recipe.

INDEX

PICTURE CREDITS

Octopus Publishing Group Stephen Conroy 5, 6, 8, 9, 25, 27, 31, 33, 37, 39, 40, 43, 45, 47,49, 51, 53, 55, 57, 59, 60-61, 63, 69, 71, 73, 75, 79, 81, 83, 85, 89, 91, 95, 101, 103, 105, 109, 111, 113, 119, 123, 124-125, 127, 129, 131, 133, 135, 137, 139, 141, 143, 145, 147, 149, 151, 153, 155, 157, 159, 161, 162-163, 165, 167, 169, 171, 173, 177, 179, 181, 183, 185, 187, 189. William Shaw 7, 20-21, 23, 29, 35, 65, 67, 77, 87, 92-93, 97, 99, 107, 115, 117, 121, 175.